QUILTING

as a hobby

by dorothy brightbill

BONANZA BOOKS · NEW YORK

Quilted linen coverlet with appliquéd floral pattern.

ACKNOWLEDGMENTS

The author and publishers wish to thank the following for their assistance and for the photographs, illustrations and patterns used in this book: Special thanks go to Marguerite Ickis for her invaluable assistance in the preparation of the manuscript and for her suggestions in the selection of illustrations and patterns used. Thanks and appreciation also go to American Home Magazine; Dover Publications, Inc. for permission to use drawings from Miss Ickis' book, "The Standard Book of Quilt Making and Collecting"; *Good Housekeeping* magazine; The Metropolitan Museum of Art; The New-York Historical Society; Alfred Rosenthal, and Paragon Needlecraft, New York City, and the Hand Quilting Dept. of Paragon Needlecraft; *Redbook* Magazine; Richard Collins and F. M. Demarest for photographs.

G

Contents

Cotton quilt made in 1822. Squares contain appliquéd flowers, stars and scenes.

An Invitation to Quilting

Anyone who can thread a needle can quilt! Anyone who likes to sew and gets satisfaction from making something beautiful and at the same time useful can make a quilt. It is fun and it's easy!

What girl or woman at one time or another has not had the urge to try her hand at making a quilt? And then, because she didn't know how to go about it or because it seemed too difficult, just let the idea go? Whether you are a confirmed "quilt fan" with a chest full of beautiful quilts and eager for one more attractive pattern, or on the verge of making your first quilt—you will find that the step-by-step instructions in this book are clearly illustrated and easy to follow.

This book will take you through each phase of a quilting operation—from simple, basic procedures every would-be quilter should know, through more advanced techniques and methods. In addition to (1) providing the beginner with a clear-cut guide to the fundamentals of quilting, the book will (2) present a variety of distinctive patterns for the ex-

perienced quilt-maker's use and (3) offer quilting suggestions in a number of traditional patterns that can be purchased, all ready for sewing. (Many women, who would otherwise enjoy making a quilt, find the cutting and other preliminary operations too time-consuming to undertake.)

A simple art, quilt-making lends itself to many pleasant interludes. It can be carried out while listening to the radio, chatting with friends, or as a bit of "pick-up work" between household chores. If the patches are cut and prepared for stitching in advance, it is a simple matter to piece them into blocks, a few at a time, and then fit them together, later. Keep the patches together in a basket with your needle, thread, thimble, and scissors, so you can work on the quilting any time you have a spare moment.

The quilt suggestions on the following pages are useful from several standpoints: some are noteworthy for their intricate beauty; others, for the history connected with them; a third group, for their value in fashion and decoration.

Every serious quilter with a little artistic acumen will delight in varying the designs suggested and in experimenting with original patterns and color combinations of her own creation.

The illustrations and suggestions in this book, along with the clear-cut guide to quilting, will give you the kind of information you need for first-class results. At the same time, it will help you to keep a bit of early handicraft flourishing in the twentieth century—giving new life to an old skill.

QUILTING TERMS AND THEIR MEANING

Let's begin with an explanation of what quilting is. The following glossary of terms and basic processes is perhaps the best way to introduce the reader to what will be described in more adequate detail later in the book.

Quilting—A method of fastening together two or (more often) three layers of fabric with a pattern of stitches. Materials used consist of a base (usually a solid section of some fabric); a filling or batting, which may be a thin layer of cotton, Dacron or Terylene; and a covering material used to "sandwich" the filling in place. The upper covering is generally a finer texture than the base, and the design used to fasten the quilt together is worked on this.

Comforter—A quilt made of fabric of the same color. It consists of three layers: a top and bottom, usually of the same material, and a fluffy "liner" of wool, Dacron or Terylene, which are all quilted together.

Counterpane—A white bed cover made of two layers of material, *without* an inner filling. The design motif is raised in relief by padding with cotton after the quilting is completed.

Appliqué—Sometimes called a "laid-on" quilt because the pieces in the design are cut from material of different colors and laid on a plain background. They are then secured in place with a fine hemming or slip stitch.

Patchwork—Usually refers to a "pieced" quilt (the pieces cut in squares, triangles or diamonds), more rarely, intricately curved pieces. These are sewn together with a running stitch, to form a design in a larger block.

Quilting Stitch—A running stitch which serves to hold together the three sections of the quilt: cover, lining and back. The stitching can follow various patterns to create different ornamental effects.

Block—Small units of a quilt (for simplified sewing). There may be four units, or blocks, or many more. The "block" (sometimes called a "patch" in a pieced quilt) can be a square, a rectangle, or a hexagon.

Setting—The sewing together of the blocks, after they have been appliquéd or pieced, to form the quilt. (Known as "setting the quilt.")

Quilting—An Ancient Art

Quilting is a very ancient craft. It was begun centuries ago in Egypt, China, and Greece. From the Middle Ages down to the present, we find examples of this fascinating art in every country where textiles were used. The practice of stitching three layers of fabric together was originally in the interest of warmth, or to produce an appropriate padding for clothing under a coat of mail. During the early part of the seventeenth century, in fact, quilting was used primarily for clothing, upholstery, and other such uses.

In parts of England and Wales, it was the custom to have an *itinerant quilter* come to the home for several weeks each year to renew the family's stock of quilts. These quilters usually brought with them their own quilting frames, on which they stretched new quilts. They also mended and rebound old quilts which were still in usable condition.

American traditions in quilting have been, perhaps, most closely identified with those of England and Holland. Influences from other countries are also reflected, however, in the quilts produced in America. Differences are more noticeable in the designs used to *ornament* the quilt, rather than in how the quilt is made.

For instance, an elaborate design suggests a French influence, which might be traced to New Orleans and the Mississippi River. In North Dakota and parts of Minnesota many quilt designs are taken from the peasant arts of Scandinavian countries. Best known and most easily recognized, of course, are the quilts made by the Pennsylvania Dutch. These are decorated in elaborate motifs and stitching, and their vivid colors—reds, greens, yellows (seldom blue)—reflect the folk arts of Bulgaria and Switzerland.

QUILTING HAS MANY USES

Let's take a beginning lesson now, in this fascinating craft, that will enable you to make the articles described on the following pages.

The technique by which a quilt is made, as

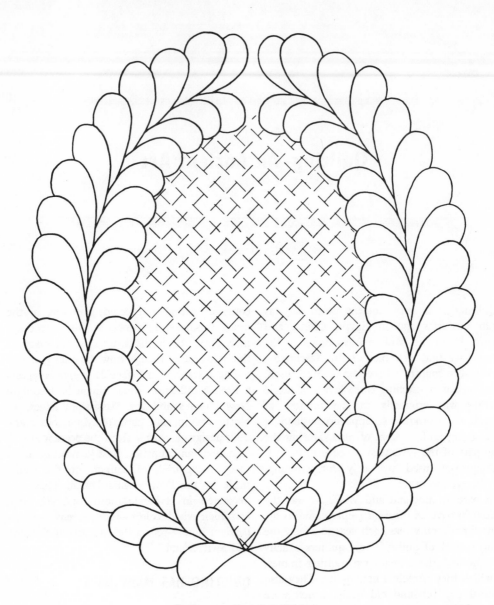

Feather wreath pattern ($\frac{1}{2}$ size).

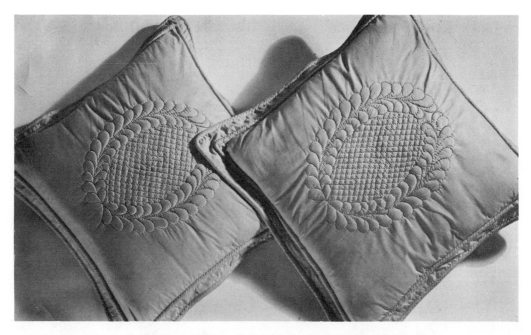

Oval feather wreath—a distinguished quilted motif for pillows.

we have said, is the fastening together of two or three layers of material by means of a decorative pattern of stitching. Careful planning and forethought are needed, however, to do this effectively.

In making quilts, cotton batting is generally used for the middle layer. In some cases, where fine stitching is not required, Dacron or Terylene is preferred. Soft cotton flannel is often used for the middle layer when small articles are being quilted. This is not the best choice, if the quilting design is to be emphasized, but it has the advantage of holding its shape if the item requires frequent washings.

Here are the basic techniques you should know, in order to quilt satisfactorily.

CUTTING MATERIAL AND APPLYING QUILTING DESIGN

The first step in making a small quilted article is to cut the material larger than the pattern, to allow for shrinkage from the stitching. Next, the quilting pattern must be transferred on to the top layer. Using a ruler as a guide, make straight lines, forming diamonds or squares, with a sharp lead pencil or piece of chalk. You can transfer any design you wish by first tracing it on paper and then puncturing a series of small holes, no more than ⅛-inch apart, along the design lines. You can use a large needle for this, or, if you wish, stitch around the lines with an unthreaded sewing machine. The holes will allow particles of

Log cabin design uses rectangular patches in contrasting shades around a central square. Narrow strips (1 inch wide) of varying lengths, laid end to end, represent overlapping logs in the cabins of early American settlers. In cutting strips, allow $\frac{1}{4}$ inch extra on all sides for seams. Baste down middle square on a square of cotton flannel. Fold under seam allowance on strips which frame middle piece, baste in place, and proceed with next row. When all strips have been basted down, secure them in place with a fine slip stitch.

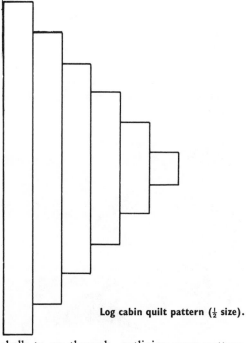

Log cabin quilt pattern (½ size).

chalk to go through, outlining your pattern. You can also purchase quilting patterns which are already perforated for transferring.

STITCHING A DESIGN

You are now ready to begin quilting. Use a short needle and white thread for the stitching since colored thread is not strong enough, and has a tendency to tangle or knot during the sewing.

Follow the lines of your design with fine running stitches, holding the needle at an *acute angle*, rather than diagonally as in other sewing. Be sure that no knots (at thread ends) show on either surface. If you cannot pull the knot up through the lining, or place it near the edge, start each new thread with a backstitch. Leave about 2 inches of thread before you make the stitch, so that you can draw it

through to the back later, with your needle. Evenly spaced stitches are important, of course, and will come with practice.

QUILTING HOOP

If you have trouble keeping the three layers of material in place during the stitching, try using a quilting hoop. You can purchase this in a department store, and although experienced quilters prefer to use a frame—the quilting hoop has its advantages. It is easily handled, for one thing, and can be moved around.

More care must be taken in using a hoop, however, when basting the three layers of fabric together. The basting stitches must run closer, so they will hold in place as you change positions in the hoop. Start the quilting in the middle of your design, and sew towards the outer edges—taking special care to keep the material smooth and free of wrinkles. (See p. 22.)

HOME DECORATION

Quilting has many applications in the home today, bringing color, design, and texture to pillows, bedspreads, draperies, chairs, curtains, and even such items as table place mats. There is no better way to create a mood with color than through the use of quilted items, such as those we shall suggest in this chapter.

Each project you undertake can add a special "extra" to your home, depending on your choice of color and fabric, and the pattern or design you select. Quilted pillows or chair coverings of silk, for example, suggest warmth and formality, while those of linen or cotton are better suited to informal use. You will find that the shadows which your stitches cast in quilting tend to soften the appearance of the

11

material. This "softened" effect is also produced by the breaking up of a plain background into many small sections. Even striped effects become less severe when quilted.

QUILTED TOPS FOR PILLOWS

Because they are small and easy to handle, pillows are excellent items with which to begin your quilting. You can use any size or shape of pillow you wish. Just be sure to allow room (at least 2 inches around) for quilting shrinkage, when you cut the material. Use Dacron or Terylene for the padding if you want the pillow top to be soft, and your design to stand out. After you have applied the quilting design to the top layer, and have basted the three layers together, begin stitching along the lines of the design. If you do this carefully, you will not need to use a hoop to hold the fabric in place.

Page 10 shows a patchwork design made with several contrasting colors. You can use fabric of silk or cotton for this design. To piece the design, begin with a middle square and sew on narrow strips the length of the square and the width of the strip. Your next row will then be made up of four strips of the same width, each longer than those in the first row. The same rule follows for each succeeding row in the cushion or block. Use cotton flannel for the filling, and then quilt along the seams where the strips are joined.

QUILTED UPHOLSTERY FOR CHAIRS

Picture shows a wing chair quilted in linen in a contemporary design of fruits. As you can see, the material covering the sides and back of the chair is quilted in a geometric pattern of parallel lines and diamonds. You can, of course,

use any type of textile in quilting a chair covering, as long as it is sturdy enough to withstand wear. If you want your design to stand out more prominently, you can add extra padding later by forcing wisps of cotton in, from the under side, with a large needle or crochet hook.

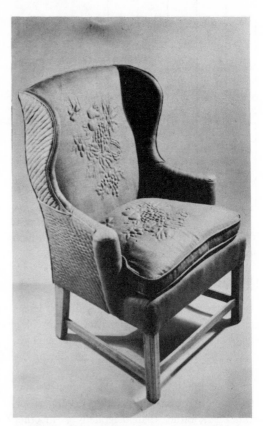

Padded fruit motif. This contemporary design is worked on linen upholstery. The same motif may be used for a quilt. See pattern and instructions on page 13.

13"

16"

Turn to page 9 for instructions on transferring a design; see page 82 for making a raised design in quilting. Note: Back of chair is quilted in parallel lines and small diamonds.

FOR CHAIR SEAT USE DESIGN UP TO BROKEN LINE ONLY. (see photo)

OMIT THIS SECTION OF DESIGN FOR CHAIR SEAT.

If you are re-upholstering a chair, remove the old cover and save the pieces to use as a pattern for a new one.

Padded fruit design for upholstery. Apply this lovely design to any plain fabric such as linen, heavy cotton or medium-weight rayon for a chair covering. Use batiste for the lining; it is soft and easily stitched. Cotton is best for the padding; it is easy to sew through and holds firm while cleaning.

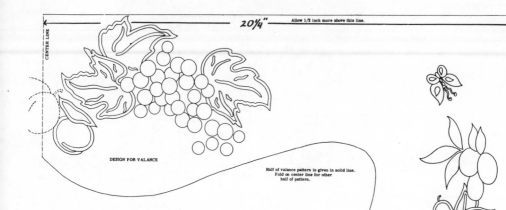

20¼"

Allow 1/2 inch more above this line.

CENTER LINE

Extend this line 1/2 inch more.

DESIGN FOR VALANCE

Half of valance pattern is given in solid line.
Fold on center line for other
half of pattern.

16"

(Above) Pattern (1/2) for Trapunto quilted valance; reverse it for the other side. Cut valance board from plywood, then cover entire front and sides with cotton batting. Trace quilting design on lining (see opposite page), then baste securely to outer cover. Sew along double lines in design with tiny running stitches, going through top fabric and lining. When design is completely stitched, fill in with wool yarn which has been threaded through a crewel needle (see page 17). Pull wool through all channels created by two rows of running stitches. Fill grapes with cotton to give a nicely rounded contour.

Linen-covered cornice with Trapunto quilted fruit motifs.

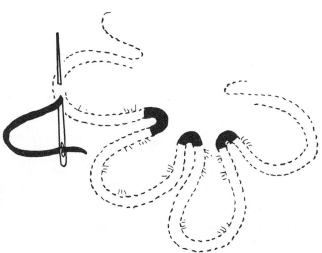

Detail of Italian-style quilting. This method of quilting is done on two layers of material, without an inner layer. The design is made by stitching two parallel lines (about ¼ inch apart) through both layers of material. These lines form a narrow channel through which a thick cord or heavy wool is pulled, with a needle working from the back.

TRAPUNTO—ITALIAN-STYLE QUILTING

Trapunto (or Italian-style) quilting is corded, and uses designs of grapevines, baskets, flower sprays, and other similar motifs, reminiscent of late American Colonial times. The stitch used in Trapunto quilting is popular in southern areas, probably because it is associated with quilting which requires *no inner lining* (suitable for milder climates). You will find many uses for this type of quilting. Trapunto designs can be applied to any number of decorative items for the home: silk coverlets, pillows, draperies, and small accessories. They also have the advantage of being suitable on almost any textile background, and are especially effective when combined with quilting. The stitching around the design tends to throw it into higher relief.

For Trapunto quilting, the pattern is sometimes stamped on the fabric that is to serve as the lining of the item to be decorated.

The design is made by running two parallel lines of stitching ¼-inch to ½-inch apart (depending on the size of cord used) through both layers of material, by working a needle from the back.

After tracing the design on the bottom layer, baste the two layers together (there is no middle layer) and sew along the lines of the design with small running stitches. When Trapunto quilting is worked from the back of the quilt where the design is stamped, and not on the top layer as in other types of quilting, you will find that your stitches on the right side are not exactly even, but the shadow cast by the raised design will make this less noticeable. If you desire fine stitching on the top layer, indicate your design on the top fabric with tiny dotted lines made with a hard lead pencil. The dots will be concealed by the quilting stitches.

As you stitch along the lines of the design, be sure to keep the width of the channel even for receiving the cord which will give the

15

**Patterns for Trapunto Designs for Chair
Seats.**

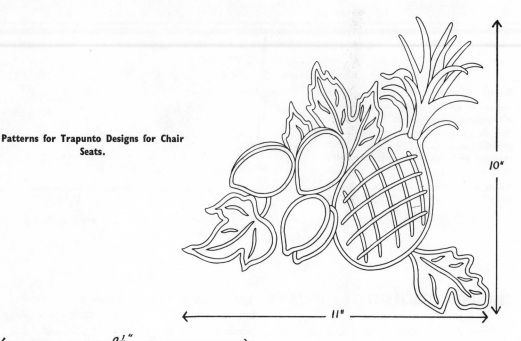

10"

11"

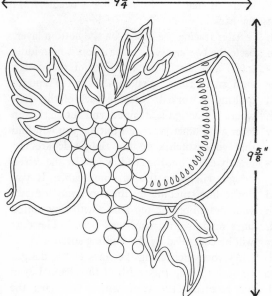

$9\frac{1}{4}$"

$9\frac{5}{8}$"

Baste top fabric and lining together
(batiste is a good choice for the lining).
With tiny running stitches, outline the
double lines of the design, sewing
through the top and lining. Fill design
with wool yarn (see opposite page).
These designs can also be used for place
mats or tablecloths. See page 9 for
instructions on transferring the design.

16

padded effect. Insert the cord (or padding) from the lining side. You may use candlewicking or soft wool yarn for the padding. Use a blunt needle with a large eye to pull the cord through the double outline of stitching which has formed a channel.

Now force the needle through the quilt lining, between the two layers of material, and thread it through the channel of the pattern. At each pronounced curve or turn, force the needle up through the lining, pull the extra cord through to the surface and then reinsert the needle through the same hole or a little farther along and continue the threading.

If the design you are using is small, with sharp turns, leave a short loop of the cord between the holes on the underside, to prevent pulling when the quilting is washed.

You can insert the needle as often as necessary, on the underside, without marking the finished design.

Trapunto quilting can be used for wearing apparel, such as bed jackets, dress trimmings and handbags. It can also be applied to cushions, dressing-table flounces, and other household-furnishing items. You can use any fabric that can be stitched with a needle and thread for this type of quilting.

 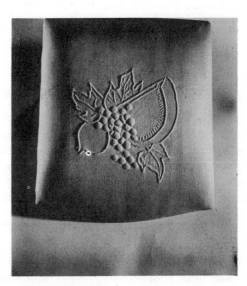

Trapunto designs for chair seats. (See opposite page.)

A quilted undercoat is easy to make—and so practical! You will want another, when you are finished, to use as a house robe.

QUILTING FOR PERSONAL ADORNMENT

Quilting has been used for wearing apparel since the days of knighthood, when it was used as protection under a coat of mail. Quilted clothing was used for warmth for many centuries—the Chinese coolie still wears heavy, quilted garments. Early Americans wore quilted vests, petticoats, jackets, skirts and bonnets to ward off the chill in houses that were heated only by open fireplaces. At first, this clothing was made of wool. Later, when houses were heated more adequately, handsome silks and chintzes were used.

Today, quilting is used for outdoor wear (ski and snow jackets, coat linings and vests). Let us not overlook, however, the special charm and individuality that quilted items offer for *indoor* use. Here are some suggestions:

WEARING APPAREL

UNDERCOATS

A quilted undercoat provides extra warmth under a topcoat on cold stormy days. It is more practical than a zipped-in lining, since it has the advantage of a high collar which gives added neck and chest protection.

Use a thin silk fabric for the top and bottom, and batting for the middle layer. Cut out the body using any basic coat pattern, and quilt the three layers of each section together, before assembling the sections into one garment. Use an all-over geometric design (diamond-shaped) for your quilting pattern. If you prefer, do the stitching on a sewing machine. Be sure to cut fabric at least 1 inch larger than pattern, on all sides, to allow for shrinkage from quilting.

A quilted undercoat of this type can also be worn as a robe. The slit at the bottom of the back can be sewn up, if the garment is to be used as a house robe.

SKIRTS

Think of a handsome party skirt, long or short, in flowered chintz (or other cotton), silk, or thin wool. Can you visualize the petals and leaves of each flower on the skirt accentuated and dramatized by quilting? To make such a skirt, line your fabric with fine cheesecloth or any pliable, thin cotton with an open weave. Baste this lining to the sections of the skirt that are to be quilted, then outline each floral unit with simple quilting stitches. When you have quilted all the floral motifs, force bits of cotton batting through the mesh of the lining into each flower and leaf, to give them a rounded appearance. Use a crochet hook or bodkin to stuff the batting into place. For this skirt, no background quilting should be used. When you are ready, use a thin silk for the lining.

Here is another skirt idea to try: one made of plain fabric—with a deep, elaborately-quilted border at the hem. Such a border gives the skirt an attractive, bouncy flair. Make the border of a patterned fabric, and then pipe it at the top and bottom in a contrasting color. If you are using a vivid print for the quilted border, you can trim the border with one of the predominating colors in the print. There are innumerable possibilities in making a skirt of this type. Variations in color and border treatment offer endless opportunities to create distinctive one-of-a-kinds that will enhance your wardrobe and earn the admiration of your friends.

To make the border, cut your fabric about 7 to 10 inches deep. Line it with cheesecloth and quilt the floral motif by stuffing the design with cotton batting—through the cheesecloth mesh. The border can then be lined with fine silk or cotton. Quilt the background of the skirt border, if you wish, with a diamond pattern. Allow about ½-inch of fabric at the top and bottom, for seams. When you have finished the quilting, slip corded piping between the flowered fabric and the lining, at the top and bottom of the border.

For added attraction, make a cummerbund! Cut a length of fabric several inches longer than your waist measurement and about 2 to 3½ inches wide. Interline this with a section of cambric (cut to the same size) and use silk or cotton in a contrasting color for the lining. Quilt with a tiny all-over diamond design. When you have finished, fit the cummerbund around your waist and cut off any surplus fabric. Be sure you allow at least 2 inches for overlap, however. Finish off the top, bottom, and ends with contrasting (or self-color) binding, and add hooks and eyes for fastening.

A vest quilted in velveteen makes a welcome addition to any girl's wardrobe. You can make such a vest in other fabrics, of course, and in any one of many beautiful shades.

VESTS

For warmth and beauty, make a quilted vest. Velveteen is an excellent fabric to use, and you can select any color you wish, of course, depending on your wardrobe. Try any of the various shades of red, blue, green and yellow that are available, which look particularly attractive in this fabric. Other fabrics you can use are Dacron or Terylene, silk, fine wool and, of course, cotton. A diamond or small-square design worked over this will give you an item you will truly be proud of.

Cut the material—top and bottom—slightly larger than your pattern (about an inch around) to allow for the quilting. The cotton batting should be shorter than the outside fabric so that it will "sandwich" in properly. Stitch together the sections of your fabric—first the top and then the bottom—then baste the cotton batting to the bottom fabric. Next, baste together the three layers (top, batting, and bottom). To be sure the layers hold properly in wider sections, make light stitches (using a fine needle and silk thread) where necessary, to keep it intact. Do this very carefully, so you do not mar the fabric.

NOTE: All basting stitches should be taken as lightly as possible, using a fine needle.

When the preliminary basting is done, snap a chalked cord over the fabric, to set the quilting guidelines. You are now ready to quilt through the three layers of fabric, using silk thread. Dust off the chalk marks, using a soft baby brush, when you have completed the quilting.

To finish off the vest, bind its edges. More elaborate fabrics call for silk binding or black silk cord which offers an interesting contrast. Bind the buttonholes with the same trimming, and sew on matching buttons or silk cord "frogs."

HATS

A quilted Scotch cap or beret makes a practical and attractive piece of headgear for cold weather. You can use any pattern to make this type of hat. Simply cut the fabric a little larger than the pattern calls for, to allow for the quilting, then proceed with its assembly and quilting just as you did for the vest. Bind the raw edges with tape or heavy ribbon.

LININGS

How about making a quilted lining that you can button on or just wear under a plain black coat? Paisley fabric is a good choice for this item, with silk lining and thin cotton batting for interlining. Proceed as you did before by sewing the Paisley sections together first, then the sections of silk, and then basting the cotton batting to the lining. Remember to allow at least an inch around for the quilting when you cut the fabric. Baste the three layers together, using light stitches, and then quilt around the Paisley motifs. Finish by binding the edges and removing the basting stitches.

BATHROBES

Buy (or make) a tailored wool bathrobe. This should be a size larger than you need, to allow for quilting "shrinkage." Make a silk lining of the same or a contrasting color and then quilt the lining to the robe in a diamond "harlequin" pattern. This item is simple to make and is a welcome gift at Christmas or birthday time.

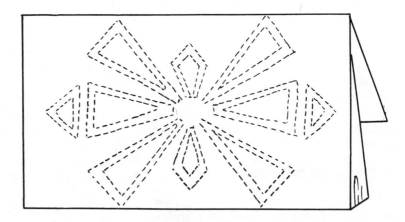

Italian quilting design on purse.

BABY BONNETS

New baby in the family? Here's a useful gift item that you will enjoy making and giving! Using a white challis, or some other soft wool, fashion a bonnet from a pattern and then line (in silk) and interline. Use little pastel flowers or animals as a quilting motif. (You can get ideas from any book for young children.) Fasten a pretty ribbon to the bonnet, for tying, as the finishing touch. You will be so pleased with the result that you will want to go on with a set—a quilted sacque, kimono, or little jacket. Repeat for those the same motif you used on the bonnet.

QUILTED ACCESSORIES

Begin a collection of old pieces of Paisley, colorful, soft woollens, and remnants of silk velvet, ribbon, and brocades. Buy "junk" jewelry at sales, and save the stones and any unusual mountings for decorating the quilted "accessories" you are planning to make. Such accessories make wonderful gifts, and can be made very quickly and easily. Here are some suggestions:

EYEGLASS CASE

To make an eyeglass case, cut out two sections of Paisley fabric a little longer and wider than the size you need. Cut two sections of silk next, to match the Paisley, and two (a trifle shorter and narrower) of cotton flannel. Baste the flannel to the lining—then baste this to the Paisley. Quilt around the Paisley design and add a scattering of "jewels" and sequins for accent. Join the two quilted parts of the case together on a sewing machine, stitching close to the edges. Trim the edges, and then bind neatly with tape or ribbon. This *boutique* gift item will be welcomed by anyone who uses eyeglasses (or sunglasses!) and wants an attractive case to carry them in.

PURSE

Here's a useful item to try! Cut out a piece of silk brocade, about 10 inches wide and 16 inches deep, and a liner of cotton flannel ($\frac{1}{8}$-inch shorter on all sides). Use silk the same size as the brocade for the lining. Baste the three layers together, and then quilt around the brocade motif with silk thread. Bind the bottom,

21

top, and 4 inches on each side with ribbon (silk or velvet) and then turn the purse inside out. Fold the bottom up 6 inches and sew the sides of this 6-inch fold to the purse—making a "pocket." This will leave a 4-inch flap at the top (bound with ribbon). Trim and finish the edges with seam binding, then turn right side out and fold over 4-inch flap. Add a jeweled pin for the clasp.

TELEPHONE-BOOK COVER

Another *boutique* item that will help solve your gift problems very nicely is a quilted telephone-book cover. To make this, cut a strip of floral fabric long enough to cover the top, sides and back of a telephone book (allowing 2 inches of extra fabric on all sides). The quilting will use up about an inch of this, leaving an inch of free space on all sides.

Line the fabric with cheesecloth, by basting it in place, then quilt around each floral motif—including stems and leaves. Remove the basting

stitches. Stuff flowers and leaves with cotton batting by forcing the batting through the cheesecloth mesh with a crochet hook or bodkin. Be sure each flower is full, firm and round.

Next, cut out a piece of cotton flannel and baste this to the quilted fabric close to the flannel edge, to prevent it from slipping. Cut a piece of bright chintz or silk the same size as the quilted fabric (for lining) and baste the three layers together: quilted top, interlining, and lining.

Trim the edges, making them straight and even. To hold the covers of the telephone book in place, sew narrow strips of grosgrain ribbon across the inside corners of the lining, about 3 inches in from each corner. Bind raw edges with the same grosgrain ribbon to reinforce the fabric. Remove basting stitches, and slip the quilted cover over the telephone book, inserting the corners of the book's covers under the ribbon strips.

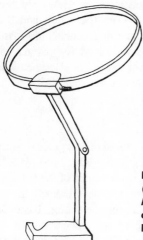

If you have no quilting frame, use a quilting hoop. (You can purchase this at a department store.) Although experienced quilt makers prefer to use a quilting frame (see page 28), hoops are easy to handle and can be moved around. Begin your quilting at the middle and work outwards.

Planning a Full Quilt

When you make your own full-length quilt, you can be as adventurous as you like. To achieve ultimate satisfaction in quilt-making, however, there are certain basic rules of color and design you should observe. The first of these is that a quilt should take its proper place in the over-all decorative scheme of a room. It should complement, and not overshadow, other areas of beauty and warmth in the room. Of course, if you prefer an all-white room with simple country furniture, then you can use brilliant colors in your quilt, as the Pennsylvania Dutch often did.

As a bed covering, the quilt plays a dramatic role. To be truly effective, however, it must harmonize in color and detail with the color and proportions of the room for which it is meant. A quilt should blend in with its surroundings. Here are some suggestions that will help you in planning.

CONSIDER THE PERIOD

The first thing to take into consideration in planning your quilt is the style or period of your furniture. If your bedroom furniture is French Provincial, for example, a quilt using a sharp geometric or Pennsylvania Dutch design would obviously be out of place. One with soft, wreathed figures in small blocks would be more appropriate. In an ornate Jacobean room, a quilted linen or wool coverlet (copied from the Orient) would be suitable.

Heavy, low poster beds look best dressed in bold appliqué or simple geometric pieced quilts. For a more conservative room, or a room with dramatic wallpaper, use a plain white quilt or counterpane, perhaps with a raised fruit and basket motif. Delicate, high posters generally call for quilts that are dainty in design and color, to accent the furniture's refinement and grace.

Many patchwork patterns are well suited to contemporary furniture, which explains their popularity.

ALL-OVER DESIGN

The size and shape of a quilt are determining factors in its design. A certain space must be filled, and to fill it properly a design is selected that will best enhance the particular quilt in question. The predominant motif of the design should stand out clearly, with everything else subordinated to it. There are several ways in which this can be done.

(1) A bold border and central motif stand out because of the open space between them. This space can be used in any one of a number of ways: alternating ornamented blocks with plain squares; separating blocks by plain narrow strips; inserting special quilted areas; and so forth.

(2) Using vivid colors for the main motifs of a design, to contrast with a background of muted tones, is another treatment. Be sure to distribute the combinations of color evenly over the face of the quilt, in using this method, to tie the design together.

(3) Repeating motif and color is the simplest way to establish unity in a design. Many of the older quilts were divided into squares, with a different motif in each block. Because each square was the same size and repeated some of the same colors, the result was pleasing.

(4) Quilt designs are usually framed by a border of some kind. This border serves as a mat, and gives the design balance and scope. Colors of the design can be carried to the outer edge of the quilt, and still conform to the overall pattern of the design, within such a border. Selection of a border is important.

SPOTLIGHT ON COLOR

A discriminating eye where color is concerned is, of course, a distinct advantage in the art of quilt-making, since color plays such a dominant role in quilting designs. Select the colors for your design very carefully. You will use and live with the quilt you are fashioning for a long time. Choose colors you will enjoy working with, and which combine well. Consideration should be given also to the mood of the design in singling out colors for it. Here are

Eagle Quilt. This dramatic appliqué design was adapted from a Pennsylvania Dutch quilt in the Philadelphia Museum Art Institute.

A

An especially effective pillow covering appliquéd in a flower basket design. (See page 41 for instructions.)

Memory Quilt. The varied designs in this lovely Friendship Quilt with cross-stitcned motifs have been highlighted by the quilting.

C

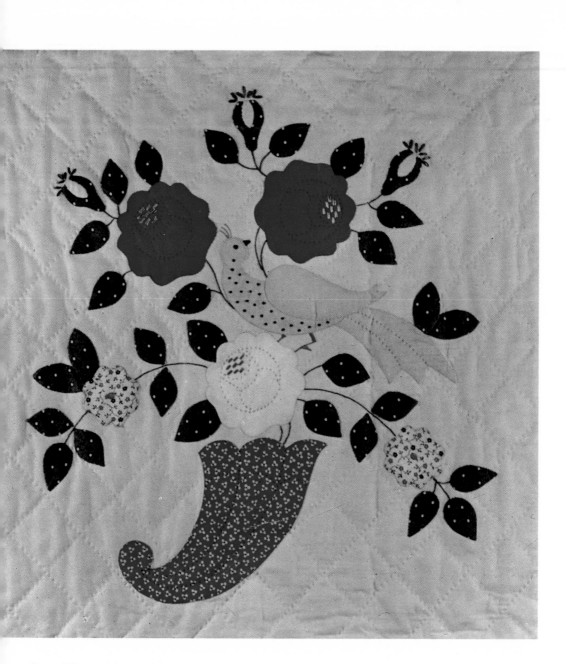

Horn of Plenty. This graceful design appliquéd in contrasting hues makes an attractive covering for pillows and quilts.

some basic principles to keep in mind in working out a color scheme for your quilt:

1—Colors in a quilt should harmonize with the general color scheme of the room in which the quilt is to be used.

2—The quilt's colors should complement the period and hue of the room's furniture.

3—They should blend in with colors in the room's wallpaper, rugs and other decorations.

4—A room's brightness and exposure should be considered. A dark room, for example, needs light or warm colors.

After studying the colors in your room, you can decide on those you will use for your quilt. Another matter to decide is how many colors and how much of each you will use. A good plan is to have: (1) one dominant color; (2) one subordinate color; (3) one or more accent colors. The accent colors should be distributed throughout the design.

A final word about color: Most people find close harmonies of related hues more restful than sharper contrasts. Such an arrangement has another advantage. Any change in the décor of your room; any variation in area rugs, change of draperies or pictures on the wall, or shifting of furniture can take place and still harmonize with your quilt.

EXPOSURE OF ROOM

A room's exposure is a factor in deciding between a warm or cool effect in any decorating plans. Rooms on the north side get no direct

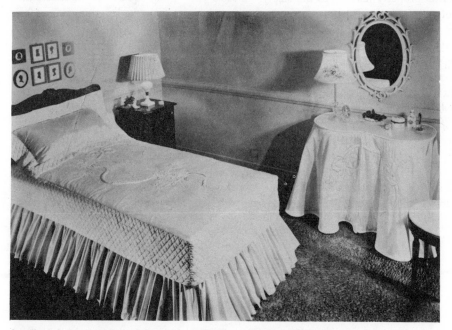

A quilted design (padded) of flowers and ribbons, for bedspread and dressing table. Diamond quilting is used on border of spread and pillow case.

sunlight and have what is called cool exposure. This is also true of rooms facing the north-east, since these get the sun only during the early morning hours. The south and southwest sides have warm exposures. Rooms which have windows on both the north and west sides have both warm and cool exposure and require less attention as far as special color effects go.

Rooms with bright sunlight can use cool colors, such as violet, blue or green. A darker room (facing north) can be brightened up with the addition of cheerful colors—yellows, oranges and reds, even a warm beige—with cushions and valances covered in the same fabric.

TAILORING YOUR QUILT TO SIZE

If your quilt is properly tailored to the size and contour of your bed, it will look right, and enhance your room. The new look in quilt fashions today sculptures them to fit the mattress snugly with mitred corners, leaving ample fabric to cover the pillows. For best results with period furniture, use a quilt with a deep enough border for a side flounce. Look through the illustrations in this book for ideas for your quilt. Notice the size and shape of the various quilts displayed and the particular designs used for each. Beds today come in standard sizes so that quilt measurements are a simple matter. The decorated area should cover the surface of the bed and extend over the pillows. The quilt's border can be deep, average or shallow, depending on the style you select. Beds of standard sizes have the following widths:

Double bed	54 inches
Three-quarter bed	49 inches
Twin bed	39 inches
Single bed	36 inches

Let's see how you can make your quilt fit one of these specifications. First, take the measurement of your bed and estimate the size and number of blocks you will need to fit the area. Draw your design pattern accordingly. If the quilt is to be made up of 14-inch (square) blocks, for example, you would need the following:

Double bed—Four squares to fit across the quilt, and five to cover its length, making 20 in all.

Three-quarter bed—The same measurements as for a double-bed quilt will fit a three-quarter bed.

Twin bed—A good division for this size bed is three blocks across and five in length—15 in all.

Single bed—Use the same measurements as given for the twin size.

Once you have determined how many blocks you will need to make your quilt, you can estimate how much fabric you will need.

Making the Quilt

Quilt-making, as our great-grandmothers discovered years ago, offers one of the richest means for creating something that is both useful and beautiful because of its pattern and color. The scope of this enormously satisfying art is greater today than it has ever been. Instead of rummaging through rag bags for scraps of fabric, as our grandmothers used to do, we can instead draw on the modern surpluses of inexpensive, washable, color-fast cottons that are available.

Whether you are an experienced sewer, or just a beginner, you will find quilt-making an easy and pleasant craft. Soon you will find yourself on the look-out for new patterns and ideas. Just watch your collection of fabric samples grow, as you pick up new pieces all the time for your "next" quilt!

EQUIPMENT

The tools needed for quilting are simple and inexpensive. You probably have most of the items you will need already, except for the quilting frame and quilt batting. Quilting equipment consists of needles, thread, a tape measure, thimble, good pair of cutting scissors, sandpaper (or cardboard) for patterns, and tracing paper. If you wish to trace a pattern, incidentally, use yellow carbon paper (sold at department stores). This will not run, smudge or streak. For the sewing and quilting involved, use short needles, about $1\frac{1}{8}$-inches long.

MATERIALS NEEDED

Quilt Top. You may use almost any fabric you wish for the quilt top: cambric, percale, fine muslin, linen, silk. Whatever you select must be smooth and soft, however. Tightly woven, heavy, or stiff fabrics will not do since it is too difficult to quilt materials of this type. Avoid using fabrics that ravel if these are to be cut into small patches. Finally, be sure all fabrics you use are color-fast and have a low degree of shrinkage. This will eliminate the problem of puckering in the laundering.

Detail of pieced quilt fastened to quilting frame. Frame consists of two poles set on end frames, braced with a bar at the bottom. Lining, batting and quilt top are basted together with large basting stitches, working from the middle outwards. The poles are wrapped with strips of muslin, to which the sides of the quilt are firmly basted (while the poles are still off the frame). The quilt is rolled on the poles (first one side, and then the other) until the body of the quilt fits the frame. The poles are then placed on each end of the frame. The ends of the quilt can be laced to the ends of the frame with crochet cord. (See page 22 for another type of frame.)

Cotton Batting (for interlining). There are several varieties of cotton batting on the market which are made especially for quilting. There is also a batting made from Dacron or Terylene which makes a fluffy quilt but is somewhat more difficult to work with, because of its bulk. This is useful in making quilts that do not require fine stitching.

Quilt Bottom (lining). Any soft, loosely woven material can be used to line a quilt. This can be plain or figured.

Binding. Ready-made bias binding can be used for most quilts. It can be white or it can repeat one of the colors in the quilt design. If you wish, you can cut out your own bias strips (from any fabric) and use this for the binding.

Quilting Thread. Use a special quilting thread (or #50 or #60) for the sewing and quilting. For very fine quilting, use #80 thread on fine fabric. White thread is best, if you can use it, since it is stronger than colored thread and does not tend to knot as easily. If you stitch the patches together on a sewing machine, use #80 thread so the seams will not be bulky and interfere with the quilting. Finally, be careful if you use *black* thread that it does not run.

ESTIMATING MATERIAL NEEDED

Let's estimate the amount of material you will need in making a quilt. To begin with, the standard length of a sheet is 108 inches (a good length for a quilt). Allow an 18-inch-wide border. If the fabric is fine muslin, it probably measures 36 inches across. Be sure you allow for any waste in the cutting of individual blocks. After determining how many squares you will need to cover the bed, estimate how much background material you will need. Include three yards to allow for an 18-inch border on each side, and an additional 54 inches for the border at each end. Add an extra yard for binding if you expect to cut the bias strips.

SETTING THE QUILT TOGETHER

Most quilts are divided into small units or blocks, to facilitate the sewing of the design, and are then sewn together when they have been completed. This is called "setting the quilt." The spacing of plain fabric used between the blocks determines the size of each block. You must therefore determine the set before you plan the pattern for your quilt. Appliquéd or pieced blocks are sometimes sewn together without a spacing, as in the Horn of Plenty. In such cases, simply cut the blocks according to the size of your bed.

There are many ways you can vary the set. The most popular method is to alternate patterned blocks with plain squares (checkerboard style). This allows the pattern in each block to stand out clearly, while the plain area is combined in the over-all quilting design.

Other patterns use a distinct top and bottom, on an angle—a tree, basket, individual flower, and so on. These are best joined diagonally, alternating with plain squares and finishing with triangles along the edge.

The use of white or solid-color strips to set blocks which have been made *before* measuring the bed size is another method that is popular. You can cut these strips in any width, as long as their size does not interfere with the design as a whole. This type of setting is sometimes called sash work.

Other Types of Sets. Old-time quilters used to set blocks that had a clearly defined top and bottom in such a way that half of them faced

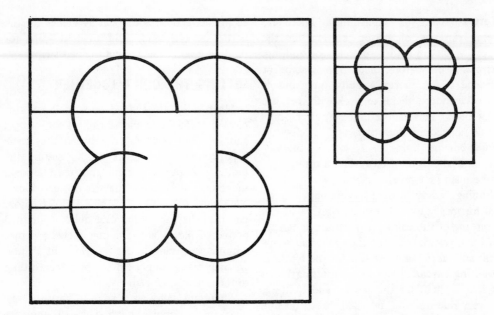

(Above) To draft a pattern by enlarging squares, begin by ruling off squares of equal dimensions on a miniature pattern. Then using a paper square the actual size of your quilt block, rule off the same number of squares, only larger. If the squares on your original pattern measure $\frac{1}{4}$ inch, and you wish to enlarge them to 1 inch (4 times as large), for example, mark off the points on the larger squares (using the 4X proportions) wherever the original crosses the lines of the smaller squares. Then connect these points, taking care to follow the original drawing.

(Right) For a large middle square, draw 2 diagonal lines across the middle of the block, then measure off the points of the square on each diagonal line. With a ruler, draw a line from each point, to form the square.

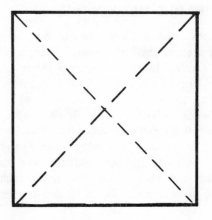

the top portion of the quilt and the other half the bottom.

Some quilt tops are divided into four large squares or rectangles. These call for an elaborate, showy pattern, usually in appliqué. Quilts of this design are especially effective on a poster bed. Some pieced blocks, such as the ones in the Orange Peel Quilt are set in an all-over design.

In setting a quilt together, it is important to have all the seams match. Sew the blocks in separate rows first, and then set them together. Add the border last.

PATCHWORK OR PIECED QUILTS

A knowledge of basic sewing, accuracy, and neatness are all you need to make a patchwork quilt. This type of quilt fits well into almost any scheme: a room with antique furniture, simple country house, or—surprisingly enough—a handsome contemporary room. The choice of a patchwork quilt for your first venture in quilt-making would be a good one. Patches eliminate the need of a quilting design, which beginners often find difficult. Stitching for this type of quilt is done around the edges of patches, rather than in large areas (as in appliqué).

SHREDS AND PATCHES

Color, as we have said, is the outstanding feature of your quilt. You can use one color with white, or many colors, depending on the effect you want. There is no limit to the range of possibilities that are open. The charm of your quilt, however, will depend on your skill in blending colors and arranging color groups so that the best possible effect is achieved.

To be sure of the proper distribution of color,

draw a sketch of the quilt you are planning to make, indicating which colors are to go where. Use crayons or water colors to fill in colored areas so that you can determine how effective your color distribution will be.

Tone values are the important thing—they tie the quilt design together, giving it unity. Combine dark, medium and light values for effective contrasts. You can use bits of figured calico for this. Grade each scrap of fabric as you take it out of your rag bag, and make separate piles of different color groups. Then cut the patches and place them in different boxes, according to their color value.

Drafting a Pattern. Probably the least interesting part of quilt-making is cutting out the units or patches. They must be cut carefully to a specified size. But first of all, you must draft a pattern.

The patterns illustrated in this book, which you may wish to copy, must, of course, be enlarged. First, study a block and see whether it is divided by square, circular or diagonal lines. If you look at the sides of the block, you can tell how many sections it has, and how these are formed.

Use a square of paper as a block pattern. By folding and creasing it, you can find the main sections into which the quilt design is divided. It is then a simple matter to divide these areas into small patches with a pencil and ruler.

Another method to try is a system of enlarging by squares. This is a popular method for getting the approximate size of each piece, and is particularly useful in appliqué. It is done this way: Cut a paper square the size of your quilt block and divide it into equal squares with a pencil and ruler. Draw the same number of squares on the design you wish to copy. (These will be much smaller.) Now transfer the design

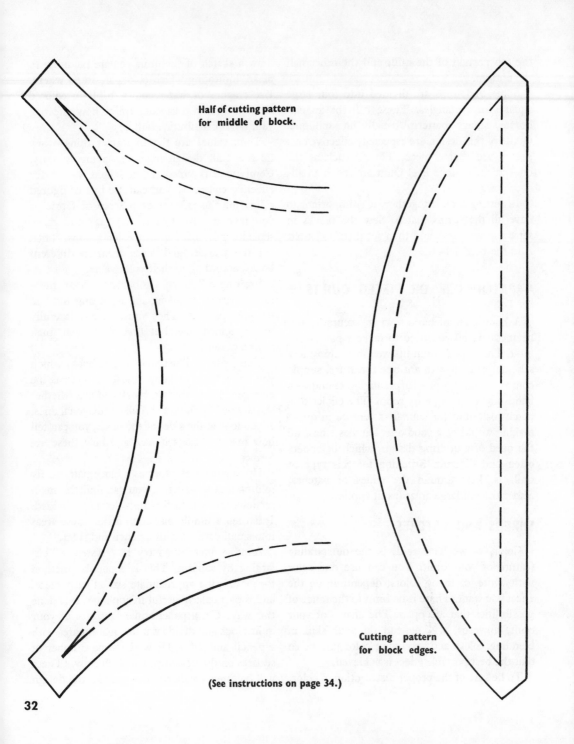

Half of cutting pattern
for middle of block.

Cutting pattern
for block edges.

(See instructions on page 34.)

32

Orange Peel quilt. This old-fashioned pieced design is most effective in one color with white.

Direction of quilting on border.

MATERIALS
16 yards of white material, 36″ wide
5 yards of dark red printed fabric
$1\frac{1}{4}$ yards of dusty pink printed fabric
Cotton batting

ORANGE PEEL QUILT

INSTRUCTIONS
Cut 1 large unit of white for middle and 4 small units of red print. Join small units to sides of large unit to form a square (block A). Make another block, using the red print for the middle and white for the small units (block B). Make 81 "A" blocks and 64 "B" blocks. Place 9 "A" blocks diagonally in row, then 8 "B" blocks in row between "A" blocks; sew adjacent sides. Place 9 "A" blocks between "B" blocks; sew adjacent sides. Continue until 9 rows of "A" and 8 rows of "B" blocks are completed. Make 16 more "B" blocks; cut these in half diagonally and insert between outer "A" blocks to straighten edges. Make 2 "A" blocks, cut these diagonally, and sew the diagonal of each half block to the free side of each corner block.

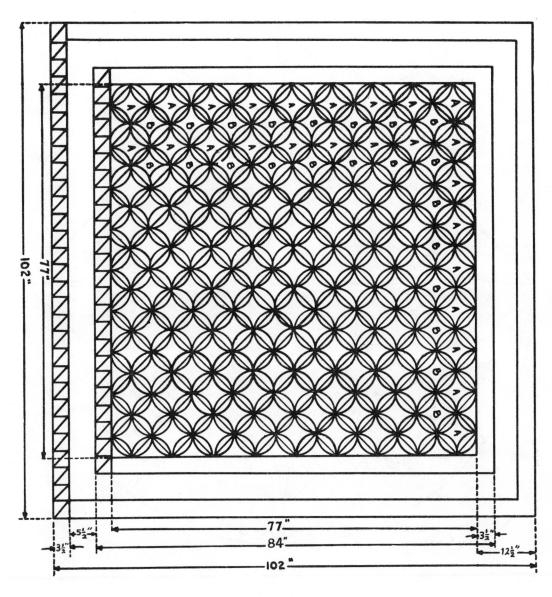

Chart of Quilt

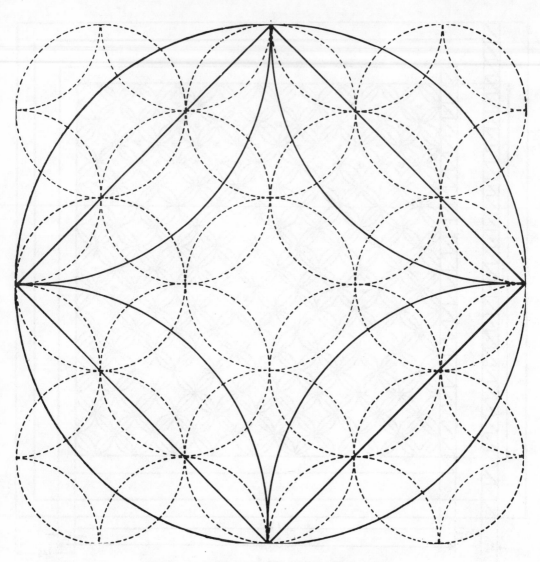

Diagram for quilting in Double Wedding Ring pattern.

to the larger block by reproducing all outlines and curves in the same places on the larger squares, as they appear on the smaller ones.

Cutting a Pattern. The best material from which to make your quilt pattern is fine sandpaper. This, laid face down on the fabric, prevents the fabric from slipping. You can use cardboard, if you prefer. If much cutting is involved, make two or three patterns since constant marking will wear away the edges.

Whether the master pattern determines the cutting or the sewing size is a matter of personal preference. Some prefer to cut along the pencil lines and then gauge their seams from this. Others cut allowing for seams by lines they have pencilled on the wrong side of the fabric. These lines serve as a guide in sewing, assuring exact finished sizes.

Cutting Material. Be sure to iron out all wrinkles from the fabric before you begin cutting. The weave of the cloth must be straight. Pull out a thread if you are not sure about its direction. When cutting patches for piecing, keep all angles sharp. Try to avoid using striped fabrics in a pieced quilt. If you must use them, be sure they all run in the same direction. Finally, remember the old adage, "waste not, want not," and cut economically!

Sewing the Patches. If you follow a few simple rules, you will save yourself the trouble of basting the patches together, before sewing them. First of all, the two pieces to be sewn together must be placed accurately and held firmly in place while the stitching is being done. All seams must be even—$\frac{1}{4}$ inch is a good depth. Sew the middle units together first, using pencilled lines as a stitching guide, and continue until the design has been completed. If you have selected a curved design, such as the Orange Peel (see page 33), begin from the middle, inside the curve, and sew first to one side and then the other. Then start at the middle of the *outside* curve, and sew in each direction. Each seam must be fastened securely at the end,

Turkey Tracks

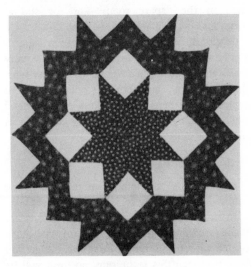

Dutch Rose

since that seam end will become part of another seam later.

As a beginning, why not make a pieced quilt block and frame it, for a dramatic picture? This does not require quilting.

The first picture is called Turkey Tracks. A bright red calico print is appliquéd on to fine white cotton. The second is called Dutch Rose or Braced Star or Broken Star and is made from a red-and-black patterned calico on a white ground. This is a pieced block. Both pictures have wide, bright red mats and narrow black frames.

⁓⁓⁓⁓⁓⁓⁓⁓⁓⁓⁓ APPLIQUÉD QUILTS ⁓⁓⁓⁓⁓⁓⁓⁓⁓⁓⁓

Appliqué gives a room its own special charm, and what home-loving woman would not like to try her hand at making a quilt of this type? Museums are filled with examples of beautiful quilts which were made during the Victorian era. These are still preserved in good condition since they were made only to be used in the "spare room"—or for special occasions.

Made during a time of rebellion against puritanical restraints, their designs were very elaborate—with large rosebuds, ribbons, fans, flower baskets, and other similar items so typical of the period. In making an appliquéd quilt, the same sewing techniques are used as in making other quilts.

WHAT IS APPLIQUÉ?

Appliqué is a method of applying one material on another, for decorative purposes, with small hemming stitches. The stitches are made after the edges of the pattern have been turned under and basted in place. Once you have mastered this technique, no quilt will be too difficult for you to make, provided you follow directions carefully. If you select your colors thoughtfully, and cut and sew the pattern with care, you will be delighted with the result when you are finished. Here are some steps to follow, if you want to try your hand at appliqué.

Drafting a Pattern. The first step in appliqué is drafting a pattern for the design. We have explained how to transfer a design on to sandpaper or cardboard, and how to enlarge a design. Be sure you leave $\frac{1}{4}$ inch on all sides of your sandpaper or cardboard pattern. You will need this for the turned-in edges. Each motif in the design will have a separate pattern, but this may be repeated several times on the same block. When you know how many times a particular motif is to be used, jot this number down on top of the pattern in question, so you will know how many to cut out.

Cutting the Fabric. To cut the fabric, lay the pattern over it and trace around the outside edges with a soft lead pencil. Cut out the various pieces and separate them according to shape and color. Be careful to keep the material straight as you work and to cut *with* the grain of the cloth. Iron out all wrinkles before you begin to cut.

Turning Down the Edges. Turn down the edges of each patch $\frac{1}{4}$ inch, and crease them in place with your thumb and forefinger. For corners and sharp turns, make small cuts or notches (about $\frac{1}{8}$-inch deep) to keep the outline of the design from stretching.

Baste the edges as you turn them, using a long loose stitch, then press flat with a warm iron. Since the basting stitches have to be removed, make the knot of the thread *on top* of the patch, so you can pull the thread out easily. (Bastings are easier to see if you use white thread on colored fabric and colored thread on white fabric.)

Flower Basket sandpaper patterns. See page 41 (Appliquéd Pillow Top) for instructions.

Flower Basket design with enlarging grid. See instructions on opposite page, and also color picture on page B.

Assembling the Design. The various parts of the design must be assembled on the block in the right place. For uniformity, square and press each block with a hot iron. Fold the block into four equal parts and the crease lines can serve as a guide for laying on the patches.

Place the large patches first, then fit the smaller ones in between. Connect the design by overlapping the patches; that is, place the edge of one above or below the edge of another. When the complete design is set on the block, secure it in place with large basting stitches.

Sewing the Patches. You are now ready to sew the patches to the background material. Use a short needle (#8) and make small hemming or slip stitches, with the longer part of the stitch on the wrong side. Barely catch the edge of the patch with your needle so the stitch does not show. Sew down first the patches that go under other parts of the design, using thread the same color as the patch.

Bias Strips. For stems and connecting lines, use bias strips. No pattern is necessary. Cut the bias strip the width needed for the design— allowing the usual $\frac{1}{4}$ inch on either side, for turning under. If you must apply a bias strip to a *curved* line, baste it first on the inside edge. You can then stretch the material out until it lies flat along the outer edge without gathering.

When you have finished the sewing, press the block on its underside with a warm iron. Use a soft pad or Turkish towel under the block, while pressing it, to keep the design from flattening.

OTHER USES FOR APPLIQUÉ

Appliqué is popular today not only in quilt-making, but for decorating other articles used in the home. This technique of applying one material to another offers endless opportunities for creative expression in the areas of color and design. Skilled needlework, of course, plays a significant part in fine appliqué.

The same graceful and intricate patterns which serve to beautify our quilts can be adapted for use in bedroom draperies, pillow cases, sheets, and cushion tops. The colors and designs used can reflect or contrast with the motifs on the bed covering.

Appliquéd Pillow Top. Let us review the procedures for doing appliqué to see how they can be applied in making the flower basket.

Study the design carefully and see if you can pick out different motifs. Mark on the pattern the number of times a particular motif is to be repeated. Then decide on the colors you will use. The large flowers in the middle include four contrasting colors. The two smaller ones, on either side, can be varied, for interest.

Make the small circles at the top of the basket all the same color. The leaves can be in several shades of green, and the tiny buds or flowers, at the outer edges, any color you wish.

Make the basket from bias strips in a basket shade (brown or yellow). If you prefer, use a color that emphasizes the decorating scheme of your room.

When the patches have been cut, and the edges basted down, appliqué the various parts of the flowers together. Begin with the middle of the motif, and work towards the outer edge.

Divide the quilting block into four sections by creasing it with a warm iron, then assemble the motifs as shown. Baste the parts in place and assemble the basket from bias strips, following the directions.

Flower stems are indicated by very narrow bias strips. For bias strips, fold cloth $\frac{1}{4}$ inch along the bias edge, then again another $\frac{1}{4}$ inch.

An appliquéd baby blanket and pillow cover is easy to make—and a welcome gift!

Baste this double fold in place and slipstitch to background fabric. Slipstitch is the tiny hemming stitch that is slipped through the fold of the appliqué seam, then into the background fabric, under the appliqué so that no stitches show on top. Be sure that the ends of the stems go under the flowers and into the basket.

CAFÉ CURTAINS

Café curtains which are translucent enough to filter out glare and offer protection from the heat and sun are a welcome addition to most bedrooms and are perfect for kitchens and dining rooms. They can be effectively decor-

ated with appliquéd designs in color, or white on white. The motifs in the design can match bed covering, wallpaper or fabric. Pick up colors used in your decorative scheme for accent.

ORGANDY LUNCHEON SETS

A striking luncheon set can be made of organdy and decorated with white appliquéd designs. For the appliqué, use white batiste (which cuts easily and will not fray at the edges). Tailor the cloth to fit your table—napkin size is a matter of preference.

Cut out flower motifs allowing $\frac{1}{4}$ inch for

seams. Baste seams to back of each motif. Baste motif onto organdy background. Slipstitch.

Prepare the border this way: Cut a white strip for the border the width you require, allowing $\frac{1}{4}$ inch on all sides for turned-in edges and several inches at each end to permit mitring the corners. Fold down the edges of the shaped side and baste, using small running stitches. Place appliqué strips along the edges of the organdy cloth (with right side of appliqué strips facing wrong side of cloth), and baste together. Mitre each corner, and cut away extra fabric.

Sew the edges together, using small back-stitches or a sewing machine. Remove bastings. Fold appliqué over to right side of cloth and press with a warm iron. Baste the top shaped appliqué to the cloth. Slipstitch appliqué in place; remove bastings and press.

NOTE: Kits are available for making such luncheon cloths, with all necessary materials and instructions in one package.

Many appliqué designs also include embroidery. The chart on pages 44 and 45 shows diagrams of the most popular stitches.

APPLIQUÉD BABY BLANKETS

Appliquéd baby blankets are attractive as well as practical. The background can be cut from fluffy Dacron or Terylene, and the motifs from contrasting colors in the same fabric. Because of the thick fabric and woolly edges, you do not have to turn the edges under as in other forms of appliqué. Simply cut out the motifs—one at a time—and baste them in place on the blanket. Sew down the edges with matching thread, using a small hemming stitch.

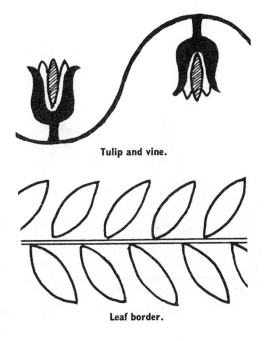

Tulip and vine.

Leaf border.

QUILT BORDERS

Borders are an important factor in quilt-making, adding size, interest and beauty. The same principles which one uses in selecting a frame for a painting apply in the selection of a quilt border. The border should sustain the pattern, but not outshine it. If you are making a solid-color quilt, however, you may reverse this rule and quilt a simple diamond or fish-scale pattern on the middle panel, and use an ornate quilted border for the sides.

A heavy, ornate border on a daintily-patterned quilt would be as out-of-place as a carved, gilt frame around a delicate painting. Here are some points to keep in mind when planning your quilt border:

Design of Border. The central color motif of the quilt should be repeated in the border.

43

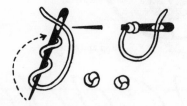

Coral or knot stitch

FRENCH KNOTS

Bring out needle, wrap thread twice round needle, hold with left thumb and take a little stitch to hold knot in place, bring needle out ready for next knot.

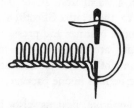

Buttonhole stitch

CHAIN STITCH

Hold the loop down with the left thumb until it is caught by the next stitch. Use as a decorative border stitch and as a padding for satin and buttonhole stitch.

Chain stitch variation

From "Complete Book of Needlework" (Ward Lock).

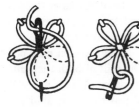

LAZY DAISY

Five or more single chain stitches worked to form daisy petals.

LAZY DAISY AND STRAIGHT STITCH

For a more solid flower work a straight stitch in a toning or contrasting color in each petal.

Feather stitch

Herringbone stitch

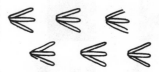

Stem stitch

Arrowhead stitch

Three straight stitches in the shape of an arrowhead. Use for light fillings.

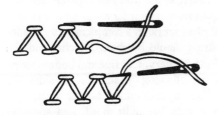

Chevron stitch

Use for lines and borders.

Cross stitch border

You can use bands of colored fabric to separate the top of the quilt from the border if you wish, and work in a variation of the central design on the border. The important thing, however, is to repeat colors from the basic design in the border. Do not introduce additional colors.

Width of Border. In size, as well as pictorial effect, the quilt border should blend in with the over-all design of the quilt. A border that is too narrow will make the central area of the quilt overly conspicuous. On the other hand, if the border is too wide it will overshadow the quilt's design and detract from its effect. A quilt which consists of 14-inch blocks should have an 18-inch border.

Three-Panel Border. Many quilts designed today have side and bottom borders only. This leaves the top of the quilt free for covering the

Examples of pieced borders

pillows. Some quilts are made with a section break before the final row of blocks at the top. This plain area is used for tucking *under* the pillows, while the blocks cover the top.

Turning Corners. Turning a corner on a border is a good test of the skill of both the quilt-designer and the quilt-maker. A neat and well-turned border is good proof of their ability.

The corners of a border should be mitred (unless the quilt is using a square for a corner motif). Adapt the particular border pattern you are using, in making the turns. The corners illustrated show how some of the old-time quilters handled this problem.

Pieced Borders. The borders illustrated were designed primarily for patchwork quilts. As you can see, they are made up of squares, rectangles, diamonds and triangles (cut from materials which match the quilt) and sewn into long rows, one or two patches wide. They are usually used as a decorative row which runs through the middle of the border strip. They are also sometimes placed at the *top* of the border to serve as a dividing line between the border and the quilt top.

If you are ambitious enough to want to sew *two* rows, either place them parallel to each other, through the middle, or put one at the top of the border and the other at the bottom. If, on the other hand, you do not wish to piece a border design at all, you can separate the top of the quilt from its border by using one or two strips of plain fabric in a complementary shade. These strips should be about 2 inches wide.

Appliqué Borders. Cut side and bottom strips for border, allowing $\frac{1}{2}$ inch on all sides for seams. Plan a continuous border design to harmonize with the quilt motif, and appliqué in same way you did the blocks. See illustration for appliqué borders on page 43.

Examples of pieced borders

Appliqué border

47

Turning a border

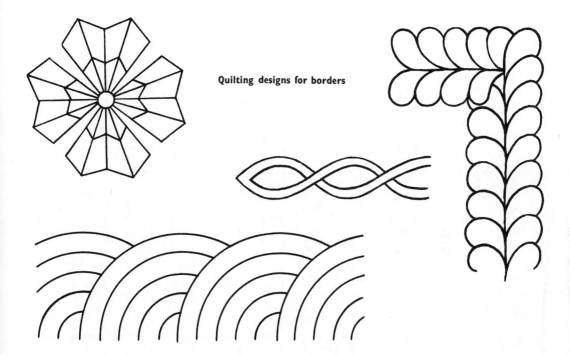

Quilting designs for borders

THE QUILTING ITSELF

Quilt-stitching is used for all types of quilts—comforter, appliqué and patchwork. When the quilt is made up of squares, quilting stitches usually cover the *plain* squares but go *around the edges* of the motifs in patterned ones. This makes the decorated areas stand out.

Quilting stitches on plain squares can follow straight or diagonal lines, and are usually worked to contrast with the appliquéd or pieced blocks. In this way, straight lines of stitching are used to contrast with a curving design, and curved lines of stitching are used where the design of the quilt is geometrical.

You will find directions for doing simple quilting on page 6. Three layers of the quilt are stitched together as described, with one exception—a quilting frame is used to hold the quilt in place while it is being worked on. The batting is fastened between the top and lining by basting it from the middle outward, and around the outer edges, as shown on frame in photograph on page 28.

MARKING THE DESIGN

When the quilt top has been completely joined and pressed, the quilting design is transferred. For a beginner, it is simplest to transfer the *complete* design.

First, determine the central point of your quilt and place a safety pin there—or use a large basting stitch in colored thread. Mark each corner the same way. If you are using a diamond pattern (the simplest form of quilting) cut a length of string that is long enough to reach from one corner of the quilt top, across the central point, to the opposite corner. Secure

All-over quilting designs.

Many hands worked on this beautiful quilt, and there was justifiable pride in the final achievement. The quilt, a prize winner, was exhibited at Hanoverdale, Pennsylvania.

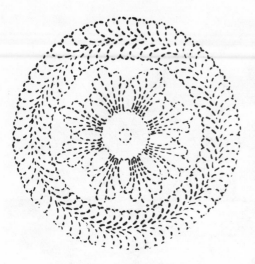

Quilting feather design.

dots. These should be no more than $\frac{1}{8}$-inch apart. Your stitching will cover the dotted lines.

You can also buy quilting patterns which are already perforated, or cut, for use with chalk or a soft pencil. If you use chalk and the design wears off, go over it lightly with a pencil.

An easy way to make your *own* quilting pattern is to draw a design on a piece of sandpaper or cardboard and go over it, with an unthreaded needle, on your sewing machine. The needle will puncture the paper in an even series of perforations on to the quilt top. If you prefer, rub a soft pencil over the punctures on the pattern. Make several copies of each pattern you use since they become worn, and the perforations become too large with continued use.

The prettiest quilts are made using *several* quilting patterns. A pieced or patchwork (appliqué) block is quilted by outlining the design and then quilting the plain blocks or bands (which join the pattern blocks) with such motifs as the "feather wreath."

Marking with Templates. For convenience, make a template, a stiff cardboard pattern in the shape of any unit in a design that is to be repeated many times throughout the quilt. There are two traditional ways to use templates. The older method is to place your template over the top layer of fabric and then scratch around its outline with a needle. When the template is removed, the scratched line should show up clearly enough for you to stitch over it. Another method, which is especially useful if the top layer is of a colored fabric, is to rub chalk around the edge of the template, leaving a chalk guide (which can be dusted off, later).

Stitching. Quilt stitching is a simple process for anyone who can sew and, as in other forms of needlework, is simply a matter of practice.

the string in this position with pins or tacks. With a sharp pencil, make a dotted line across the quilt top, using the string as a guide. The dots should be $\frac{1}{16}$-inch apart for fine quilting, and $\frac{1}{8}$-inch apart for less fine quilting. Make a series of dotted lines the same way on each side of the first line (an inch apart) until the entire top of the quilt is marked with diagonal lines going in one direction. Repeat, with dotted lines going in the opposite direction, to form diamonds.

Another method you can use is to chalk a string with plumber's (or quilter's) blue chalk. Tack the string in opposite corners, as described, and snap it crisply against the quilt top. This gives a sharp, clean line—although it tends to rub off during the quilting. You can transfer any design you wish to a quilt top by tracing it first on paper and then piercing the paper repeatedly with a sharp pencil, to reproduce the design on the quilt top in a series of

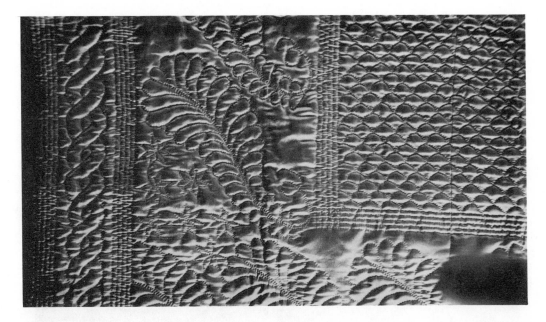

Several quilting motifs are used in this exquisite silk quilt. The middle, a tiny shell pattern, is framed with a band of straight-row quilting. A section quilted in feather plumes follows, bordered in straight-row quilting, then a cable strip, and finally, the edge is finished in straight-row quilting.

Your first attempt should be straight lines—with curves and "feathers" coming later.

In quilt-stitching, the first thing to remember is that it is easiest to quilt *towards* you. Take very fine running stitches (old-time quilters boasted 20 stitches to the inch), using a short needle, and thread (#50) not longer than 16 inches. Hold the needle at an acute angle as you sew, keeping the fabric in place with the thumb of your opposite hand. Some people quilt while keeping their left hand *under* the quilt and using a forefinger where the needle touches the fabric. Be sure to protect your fingers from needle pricks with adhesive tape or a commercial fingertip.

BINDING A QUILT

Binding is the finishing off of raw edges on an otherwise completed quilt. You can do this by (1) turning the edges of the top back, over the lining, and sewing these down with hemming stitches; (2) turning the narrow edge of the *bottom* layer over the *top* layer, and hemming it; or (3) binding the three layers together with standard bias tape (sold at department stores). Another and better method is to cut your own bias strips from a matching or contrasting piece of fabric used in your quilt, and use them to bind together the edges of the three layers. This usually makes a more effective binding since it matches (or contrasts with) the colors in your quilt. It also withstands fraying better than commercial tape, since it is sturdier.

53

An example of a "quickie" quilt, that can be used as both spread and coverlet.

"Quickie" Quilts

These quilts, designed by the author, fill a need by young marrieds with small children for simple, but dramatic, bed coverings that can be used both as spread and coverlet. They are simple to make, and easy to care for.

DIAMOND PATTERN

Select a firm, but soft, white fabric—such as cotton broadcloth or poplin for the top, and a soft batiste for the lining. Use Dacron or Terylene batting for the interlining. This makes a fluffy and thick (but light-weight) quilt, and is suitable for the type of quilting stitch and thread we shall use.

Since most white cotton fabrics come in 36-inch widths, select a 36-inch width for your central panel. Split another length of the 36-inch width fabric in half (making two 18-inch widths) for joining on either side of the central panel. Be careful, in joining the side pieces, that they are attached evenly and smoothly to the central panel (so there are no wrinkles or puckers). Make the lining the same way, and then press all seams and the fabric top.

Spread the top fabric out on the floor and tack down the corners and the middle of each side, to hold it smooth and straight. Rub a piece of string (long enough to reach from one corner diagonally across to the opposite corner) with blue tailor's chalk. Fasten a tack or pin to each end of the string and insert these in opposite corners of the fabric, being sure to keep the string taut. Snap the string so it marks the fabric, then repeat with another line 6 inches away from either side of the first line. (Re-chalk the string as necessary). Continue this procedure across the entire top of the fabric, moving in the same direction. When the diagonal lines in one direction are complete, repeat, going in the opposite direction. Remove the pins or tacks, and gently lift the marked fabric. If some of the chalk rubs off, go over the line lightly by hand. Lay the lining out flat on the floor and spread the Dacron or Terylene batting over it evenly, trimming away any surplus.

You are now ready to baste the top, middle and bottom layers together, from the middle outward, using large basting stitches. Handle the fabric as little as possible, so as not to disturb the blue chalk. Now place the basted quilt in a quilting frame, being sure the middle of the quilt is in the middle of the frame.

Starting from the top of the quilt, quilt along the chalked lines, using heavy Pearl cotton and a darning needle. Make each quilting stitch $\frac{1}{2}$-inch long on the face of the quilt, and $\frac{1}{8}$-inch long across the bottom layer (lining). This will provide a series of $\frac{1}{2}$-inch-long stitches ($\frac{1}{8}$-inch apart) on the face of the quilt. Keep your stitches straight and even. When you have finished quilting half of the lines going in one direction, move the quilt in the frame and continue until you have quilted all the lines going in the same direction across the face of the quilt. To form the diamonds for your pattern, simply *reverse* the process, quilting back across the lines you have already done, in the opposite direction. When you have finished all the diamonds, remove the quilt from the frame, trim off any scraggly edges, and bind. This type of quilt is handsome, useful and relatively simple to make.

CIRCLE QUILT

Here is another design to try that would be suitable for a youngster's room. It is made of interlocking circles, and uses a chain stitch for the quilting. First, mark off your quilt top in 14-inch squares. Then mark each line of each square with interlocked circles (the size of an orange) this way: cut a paper pattern 18 inches square and draw a 14-inch square in the middle. Be sure all lines you draw are straight and even. Using a teacup for a guide, draw interlocked circles directly over the middle of each line of the 14-inch square. Interlock the circles about an inch at the top and bottom. You will have to adjust this, to get an equal distribution of circles around the square.

Transfer this design to the quilt top, stretching the fabric out on the floor as you did in making the diamond pattern. Mark off 14-inch

squares on the quilt top, using chalked string. Tack the string first vertically and then horizontally across the quilt, and pin the paper pattern directly over each line of each square. Pierce the interlocked circles on the pattern (about $\frac{1}{4}$-inch apart) using a sharp pencil. Move the pattern to the next square, and repeat. You will see that once the first square has been transferred, only three sides of all the others need to be pierced, to complete the square. For the quilting, quilt only the *circles*. *Do not quilt the chalked lines which form the squares.* These lines—which are only guides for the circles—will be brushed off once the circles have been quilted. Use a simple chain stitch, making each stitch about $\frac{1}{4}$-inch long, using heavy Pearl cotton. When you have completed the stitching, brush off the remaining chalk marks using a soft baby brush. Trim the edges, and bind with bias tape.

VARYING THE DESIGN

Another pattern you may wish to try is one made of 6- or 8-inch squares which are quilted in old-fashioned feather stitching, using heavy Pearl cotton.

You can vary the color scheme, of course, of any of the quilts described here, to suit your own special needs and taste. A quilt in a solid-color background (or white), for example, can be quilted and bound in a contrasting shade, to dramatize the quilt's design. A patterned quilt, on the other hand, may be better suited to white or colored quilting thread and binding —or you may wish to repeat one of the colors in the fabric. There is no limit to the possibility of color combinations you can use, provided the colors you select for your quilting and binding enhance the over-all design of the quilt.

Examples of cross-stitched designs (see page 59).

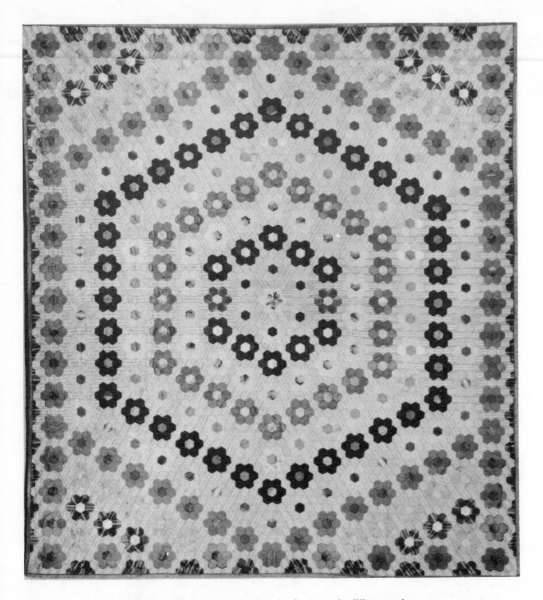

Mosaic quilt uses concentric bands of rosettes in different colors.

58

Quilts of Distinction

CROSS-STITCH QUILTS

The cross-stitch quilt is an easy, fast way for the newcomer to create a design. This type of quilt comes pre-stamped in a variety of carefully-chosen designs to complement all types of decorating schemes. See examples, in color pictures. Its cross-stitched top looks like fine appliqué, when completed.

Instead of the more usual block (or squares), these quilts come in panels, with several blocks stamped on each panel. There are two panels for a single size, and three for a double-bed size. You can make this type of quilt top in either of two ways:

(1) Each panel can be embroidered separately (for ease in handling) and then joined when the embroidery has been completed—except for any cross stitches that may be needed on the joining lines. It is important to use an embroidery hoop, while working the cross stitch, to keep the fabric evenly stretched.

(2) Panels can be joined *before* embroidering them. This procedure is recommended for the beginner, since it is easier to match crosses on joined seams using this method. Its disadvantage is that the fabric is bulky to handle. A large, round embroidery hoop will be helpful in keeping the fabric taut, making it easier to embroider uniform stitches.

JOINING PANELS FOR DOUBLE QUILT

Pin the three panels together, matching the numbers stamped on the panel. Match the borders, quilting lines and crosses carefully where they meet at seams. Slipstitch the seams together by running your needle through the fold of seam on one panel, beneath the point at which both panels meet, and on to the fold of seam on the other panel. Repeat, making your stitches $\frac{1}{16}$-inch apart. Be sure all stitches are concealed in the folds of seams. Sew with the right side facing up so you can watch your work as you go along. If necessary, remove the pins to straighten the crosses. Also remove pins

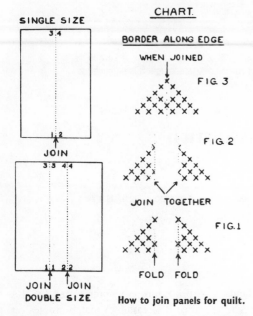

SINGLE SIZE

BORDER ALONG EDGE

WHEN JOINED

FIG 3

JOIN

DOUBLE SIZE

JOIN   JOIN

FIG. 2

JOIN   TOGETHER

FIG. 1

FOLD   FOLD

How to join panels for quilt.

which are no longer needed to hold the fabric together, as you go along. When you have finished all the stitching, iron on the right side, over a pressing cloth.

Single-size quilts are made the same way, except that two panels, instead of three, are used.

CROSS-STITCH EMBROIDERY

Cross-stitch embroidery is most effective when it is worked properly. Work the crosses in one direction, from left to right, one row at a time. Finish by working back across the same row, from right to left. Make all stitches the same length, being sure they touch where they meet.

Floss (thread) for cross-stitch embroidery comes in six strands, twisted together. Generally, two or three strands are separated for the embroidering. (For a heavier effect, you can use

four strands.) When you have finished, iron (on a flat, padded surface) using a slightly-dampened cloth over the embroidery—and allow to dry thoroughly.

Quilt, as previously instructed.

THE MOSAIC QUILT

This quilt is also known as the honeycomb quilt because of its resemblance to the waxen cells made by honeybees. The cover is made up of hexagon-shaped (six-sided) patches which have been pieced together to form an all-over pattern. Occasionally, this type of quilt has a central motif. (See page 58.)

For the "modern" quilt designer, here is an old-fashioned Flower Garden quilt in an all-over pattern. The central hexagon of each block should be a yellow fabric. The next two rows of hexagons are in a different printed fabric—blues, pinks or yellows. Then comes a surrounding row of hexagons in shades of green, to represent the foliage or leaves. Finally, a row of solid-white hexagons frames this central design—forming a path between the flower beds in this charming quilt, known in Colonial America as Martha Washington's Flower Garden quilt.

DOUBLE IRISH CHAIN

This popular old pattern is made by piecing together (diagonally) small squares of alternately dark and light fabrics in strips that criss-cross over the quilt's surface. These strips are pieced together with plain quilted blocks of the same size, giving an all-over effect of a solidly pieced quilt. Use two shades of the same color for the patches, or use two harmonizing colors.

A simple method of piecing this quilt is to

Double Irish Chain is a pattern of small squares of fabric in diagonal strips that criss-cross over the quilt's surface. The pieced strips are set together with plain background blocks (quilted the same size as the pieced strips) to give the effect of a solidly-pieced quilt. Two tones of the same color can be used for the patches, or two harmonizing colors.

piece a block of 25 squares and then set these together with a plain white block, appliquéing a colored square in each corner. To do this, arrange the color squares in each block as follows:

Row 1—light, dark, white, dark, light.
Row 2—dark, light, dark, light, dark.
Row 3—white, dark, light, dark, white.
Row 4—repeat row 2.
Row 5—repeat row 1.

Cut a white block the size of the pieced blocks and appliqué a dark square in each corner. When the blocks are set together, they will form the Irish Chain.

OUTDOOR-INDOOR QUILT

Now it is time to design a quilt especially for use in a bedroom that has a large, windowed area overlooking a garden or terrace. Let us bring a little of the garden indoors, using its flowers, colors and textures.

Appreciation of nature was one of the attributes of the early quilt-makers, as is shown by their efforts to copy various forms of leaf and flower. The next time you design a quilt, why not do as they did? Look out of your window and be inspired by what you see in the garden. You may see a yellow primrose, a

62

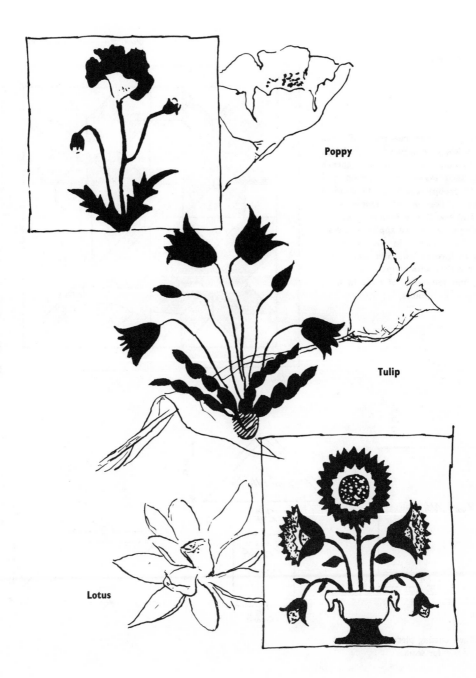

Poppy

Tulip

Lotus

Kansas Sunflower.

A striking, gay pattern—the sunflowers in soft yellow with brown "eyes." Stitch petals together as shown, add corner square, then make second group and sew both groups together; add triangle between. Make second four-petaled group and sew this to first section; add remaining triangles and appliqué "eyes" on. Appliqué stems on fourth block, leading to flowers, and add leaves. Set blocks together with strips of green or yellow, and trim edge of quilt in both colors.

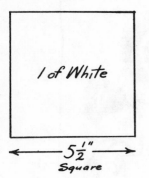

1 of White

5½" Square

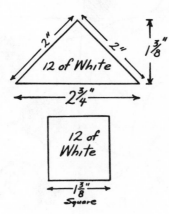

2" 2"
12 of White
1⅜"
2¾"

12 of White
1⅜" Square

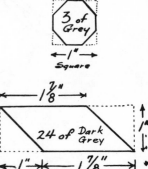

3 of Grey
1" Square

1⅞"
24 of Dark Grey
1"
1" 1⅞"

When cutting pieces, allow for seams.

64

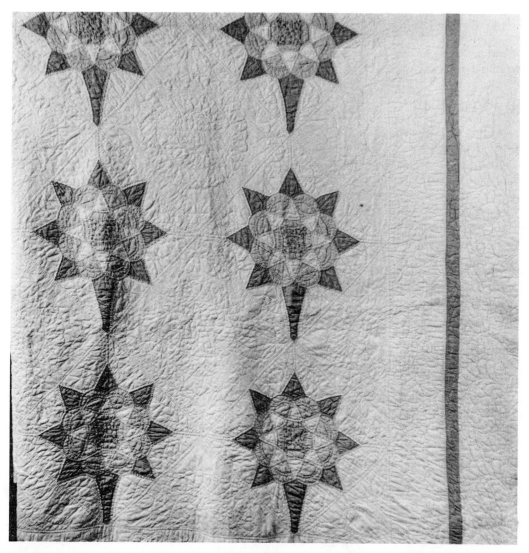

One of the most beautiful of the pieced quilt patterns, the Harrison Rose is done in very fine quilting and made of several feather motifs with tiny hearts.

pink peony, a purple iris, a rose, or a day lily, just to mention a few. If you prefer, make a basket pattern and fill it with a variety of beautiful flowers copied from your garden.

HAWAIIAN QUILTS

Quilting has been a craft on the tiny Hawaiian Islands for over a hundred and fifty years. It is especially interesting to study these quilts, as they show the beginnings of the craft among a primitive people excelling in beauty of design.

Quilts made in the Hawaiian Islands today have two distinct decorative characteristics. Their most prominent feature is a large, all-over motif which is cut out and applied to the background.

The second distinguishing feature of these quilts is the single-color tone used in the cut-outs which are applied to contrasting backgrounds.

Native designers use the fruits, vegetation, and tropical surroundings in which they live for inspiration for their designs: palms, pineapples, seaweed, coral, and lush tropic flowers.

To cut out the large, quilt-sized motifs, the islanders first fold the fabric they are using into segments leading to the middle of the quilt. With a sharp knife pressed against a firm, stiff pattern, they then cut through all the layers—producing the all-over cut-out motifs.

To make these designs practical for use in modern sewing rooms, the Hawaiian techniques must be adapted, and their patterns scaled down to one-fourth the size of the original. Simply make a pattern for one-fourth of your quilt, cut it out, and then repeat this pattern four times to make the four sections of your quilt. This makes the work of appliqué much simpler, because you can hold and work with these smaller sections easily.

Color contrasts, both bold and harmonious, can be used. If you want more subtle color tones, use two sheets—one white and another in a pastel shade—then follow the instructions given for appliqué in applying a design.

Pattern section of Hawaiian quilt shown on opposite page.

Hawaiian quilt appliquéd with all-over motif. Middle unit is cut from one piece of fabric; border is cut separately.

Hawaiian quilt pattern.

Crazy quilt pillow top made from scraps of silk and velvet. The patches are sewn on a plain silk top and decorated with feather stitching.

CRAZY QUILT

Crazy quilts consist of an all-over design pieced together from different scraps of fabric, regardless of size or color. With the scarcity of fabrics in earlier days, women saved all usable parts of worn, woollen clothing and pieced these sections together in "crazy" fashion—usually on an inner lining since this helped hold the pieces in place while they were being sewn. On more elaborate quilts, yarn was sometimes used to join the pieces in simple embroidery stitches.

Later, the lowly crazy pattern was elevated to the parlor by substituting scraps of silk and velvet for the worn, woollen pieces. This was used as a throw for the couch, or as a slumber robe. Sections of fabric were fastened together with fancy stitches, and silk floss was used

instead of yarn. The patches were often decorated in flowers, fruits, hearts and hand-painted designs.

If you like to combine colors, and have some knowledge of embroidery, you will enjoy making a crazy quilt. It is not difficult, once you know how. Here are some easy steps to follow in making a quilt of this type:

(1) Collect silk scraps (men's discarded neckties are excellent) and sort them according to lights and darks. Iron out all wrinkles.

(2) Cut out a foundation block (16 inches square) of muslin or cambric—using 20 blocks

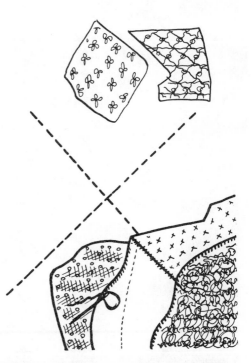

To place patches in a crazy quilt, start from the corner of the block and work to the left, as shown. Stitch the left sides of the patches after the next patch has been laid in place under the seam.

CRAZY QUILT

for a full-size quilt. For added warmth, include batting the size of the block, and baste this to the foundation. (You can buy batting, with a glazed surface, in sheets.)

(3) Begin placing the pieces of silk by setting the first patch in one corner on the padded surface. Baste this in place, and then repeat in the remaining corners. Fill out the rest of the block by laying patches which have two edges basted down on top of the raw edges of those already in the square. Sew down all patches with hemming stitches, and cover the seams with embroidery.

TWO QUILTS FOR A BOY'S ROOM

Tumbling Blocks. This is an old pattern, and is usually made of plain and printed calicoes. The blocks are set alternating plain and printed colors. (See illustration for how to do this using dark and light blocks.) Try exchanging bits of fabric with your friends for a greater variety of color and design.

Wild Goose Chase. This bold design is wonderful for a boy's room. It is not difficult to piece, and has enough pattern to make it interesting to work on. In red and white, with a blue background, it could be the focal point of a room. (See pattern on page 72.)

Cut all pieces following the size on the pattern pieces illustrated. Be sure to allow ¼-inch extra on all sides of each piece, for seams. To sew, first make a corner strip of 4 white triangles ("geese") filled in with red triangles. There are 8 small triangles and 1 large red triangle for each strip. Sew a large blue triangle along each side of this strip. Then sew a white square on the inside end of the strip.

Make 3 more strips of "geese" out of red and white triangles and sew these to the white square of the first unit. Stitch the remaining blue triangles in place, and iron the seams flat. Set the blocks with 2-inch strips between each block—window-sash style.

The average bed will require 3 blocks across the top and 1 block for each side, totaling 5, and you will need 6 blocks for length. This means 30 blocks in all.

Add a 6-inch-wide blue border on both sides and at the bottom. When you have joined the blocks to make the top, add cotton padding and a lining and baste the three sections together. Quilt around each piece of the design, and then quilt the border with a simple vertical design, such as the cable.

Tumbling blocks—a welcome pattern for use in a boy's room. Alternate vivid colors with contrasting prints for a cheerful effect.

Wild Goose Chase.

←——— 12″ ———→

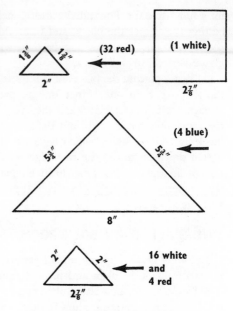

(32 red) ← (1 white)

1 3/16″ 1 9/16″

2″

2 7/8″

(4 blue) ←

5 3/4″ 5 3/4″

8″

16 white
and
4 red ←

2″ 2″

2 7/8″

When cutting pieces, allow for seams.

(Right) Bear's Track. Fold block to form middle square and 4 rectangles. Divide each corner square into 1 large square, 8 small triangles and 1 small square.

(Left) Robbing Peter to Pay Paul. Fold block to form 9 squares. Divide each corner square into 6 triangles and 1 small square. Divide middle blocks into 1 large triangle, 2 small ones and 1 rectangle. Middle square is plain.

Secret Drawer and (right) Delectable Mountains. Both designs are pieced. Use enlarging squares to draft the patterns.

Quilting in America

We like to think of quilt-making here as an American craft, especially the pieced variety which pioneer women cut so painstakingly from bits of material and sewed into various designs. The hundreds of quilt patterns they left serve as a testimonial to their ability to conceive and execute original designs in quilts which are both beautiful and functional. In reading over the names of the various patterns, one can almost say that the life of America is written in her quilts. Many of the patterns reflect the social, political, and religious thinking of its people. To this, one can add historical events, geographical areas, native flora and fauna, and innumerable other subjects. Listed here are the names of some of these quilts. From them, you can span a century of American history:

Whig's Defeat, Westward Ho!, Star of the

Ohio Star. Divide block into 9 equal squares. Five squares are plain; the remaining 4 are divided into 4 equal triangles.

shades of several colors were arranged in swirls around the star. The Morning Star was made in shades of yellow, orange, pink, and lavender —all the colors of the sunrise. Sometimes, the colors of the rainbow were used instead.

Other star patterns bear the names of various states. Whenever a new state was added to the Union, a new star appeared in the blue canton of the flag. Similarly, the quilters of America would design a new star pattern, and christen it with the name of the new state. The star of North Carolina and that of Tennessee are among the better-known star patterns. The Texas star is the *smallest* star in the group!

Handicrafts, like other types of human effort, are popular in cycles. As the popularity of one reaches a peak, another's wanes. The fad—in short—wears out, until it is revived again. This is not true of quilt-making, however. Quilts have always been with us. Women are making them today everywhere. The fact that the

West, Log Cabin, Old Hickory, Rocky Road to California, Ohio Rose, Rebel Feather, Pine Tree, Bear's Paw, Big Chief, Little Red School, Lincoln's Platform, Old Tippecanoe, Fifty-Four-Forty-or Fight, White House Steps, Kansas Star. And these are only a few!

The star was a popular subject for patchwork quilts—probably because the units in a block were made up of triangles of the same size and were therefore relatively easy to make.

STAR PATTERNS

Based on variations of the diamond and square patterns, star patterns outnumber all other designs. One of the oldest-known patchwork-quilt patterns is the "Star of LeMoyne." The LeMoyne brothers were given a grant of land in 1699 known as Louisiana, and in 1718 they founded the city of New Orleans. A number of the quilts made during that period were ornamented with a single star made up of hundreds of small diamonds. Light and dark

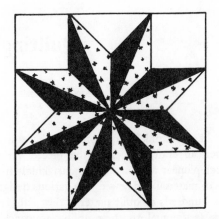

Star of LeMoyne. Fold block across middle each way and divide into 9 equal squares. Lines of squares give triangles' points. Use figured or plain white material.

74

patterns and designs have varied little in over a hundred years is the best proof of their durability and charm. Only the colors have changed to any extent and this has been due, of course, to improved techniques for making fabrics color-fast, and to other modern innovations in dyeing.

To make useful and beautiful items from the coarse fabrics that were available was an everyday accomplishment of pioneer women. In Colonial days, every bit of cloth used had to be brought to the colonies from England and France, in sailing vessels. Because these materials were scarce, not a scrap was wasted. Not all quilts were made out of small pieces, however. Wealthier citizens in New England and some Southern states were able to buy fabrics in quantity—so that larger sections of material in various shades could be used to work out original and interesting designs. This practice developed earlier in the South than in New England, and many of the finest examples of old quilts found in museums today were done by mistresses of Southern plantations. A large percentage of these early quilts were made in pink and white, a popular combination in that period.

1 8 5 3

Many of the designs used in the early quilts reflected the patriotism that enveloped young America, following the Revolution. The American eagle, adopted by Congress in 1782 for the Great Seal of the United States, became a patriotic emblem. The works of leading sculptors and artists served as models for innumerable craftsmen who adopted such emblems in decorating their carvings, furniture, glassware and textiles. The housewife, too, used such emblems as the eagle for the central motif in quilts, hooked rugs and other items she was making for home use.

For many years, the American Indian served as a symbol of this continent. As the nation developed, new symbols appeared. Besides the American eagle, there were the Shield (or Emblem), the Liberty Cap, and two notable figures: Liberty and Justice. But none of these was especially suitable for ornamenting a quilt. "Thirteen" became the magic number for symbolizing the Thirteen Colonies. When a

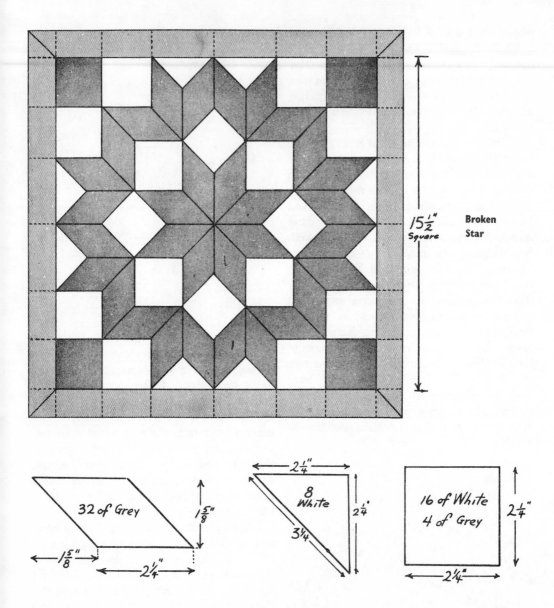

$15\frac{1}{2}"$ Square

Broken Star

32 of Grey — $1\frac{5}{8}"$ — $1\frac{5}{8}"$ — $2\frac{1}{4}"$

8 White — $2\frac{1}{4}"$ — $2\frac{1}{4}"$ — $3\frac{1}{4}"$

16 of White 4 of Grey — $2\frac{1}{4}"$ — $2\frac{1}{4}"$

When cutting pieces, allow for seams. Use a striped fabric, and have stripes run from one point of diamond to the other. Make middle star by joining 8 pieces, as shown. Complete block by adding pieces around star. Illustration is for a cushion. To make a quilt, omit edging and sew blocks together. For contrast, make corner squares in a solid color and trim quilt border with a 4" strip in same color.

large eagle was used as the central motif on a quilt, therefore, thirteen stars were often used with it, as background. These were sometimes cut out of contrasting material and appliquéd to the quilt. More often, however, they were quilted into the design. The illustration on page 75 shows one of many groupings used for the stars. The other illustration includes lines for depicting the body and wing feathers of an eagle, for a quilting design.

The number thirteen was not only indicated by the use of stars, but also by repeating any motif of the design thirteen times. Early pressed-glass patterns, for example, used either stars or some other motif—such as hearts,

flowers, fruit, and other items of this nature— repeating them thirteen times in whatever arrangement looked best with the central motif. The quilter adopted similar designs for use on quilts.

The quilt illustrated (color p. A) combines this early attempt at symbolism with the folk art of the Pennsylvania Dutch. Notice the thirteen stars placed over the body of the eagle (the central motif). The eagle is enclosed in a large heart—a folk symbol. Leading out from this are thirteen branches with buds and flowers. The design is executed in vivid colors— reds, yellows and browns—which contribute further to the folk quality of the quilt.

"Snowflower" quilt. Modern Pennsylvania Dutch design adapted for contemporary decorating.

78   "Four Continents" design. Cotton panel, printed in red. (France, 18th century, Jouy.)

TEXTILES USED IN OLD QUILTS

To understand and appreciate Early American quilts fully, some knowledge of the textiles used in them is necessary. The first quilts—like those in England—were made from large pieces of chintz or calico, on which a design in one or more colors was printed. If the fabric was made before the seventeenth century, it probably came from India or Persia, since both the English and French found it more economical to import cotton that had already been woven than to own and operate their own looms.

The patterns used on Indian prints were large and bold, and colors in the design were generally painted by hand. The most typical pattern motifs were flowering trees, cypresses, poppies, roses, and other floral figures. Animals, real as well as imaginary, were used and even more popular were the bird forms, such as peacocks and hawks.

Since designs were applied to the cloth by hand in India (rather than being printed from a block), the size of the pattern was of little concern. Many of these Indian textiles, therefore, were ornamented to resemble the Oriental rugs which were so popular in Colonial homes. Designs like the Tree of Life were large enough to cover an entire quilt top. These cotton textiles were known as palampores, and are still sold in the markets today. Extraordinary fabrics (Paisley) were also made from the wool of Cashmere and Angora goats.

For the next hundred years, England and France imported plain white cotton fabrics only, so that they could apply their own ornamentation. England imitated the rich floral designs of the Orient but personalized them by substituting her own native flora and fauna. But it was in France, through the efforts of one man, Christophe-Phillippe Oberkanph, that cottons were most successfully decorated and popularized. It was M. Oberkanph who designed the all-over patterns (on toile) of pastoral scenes, with cherubs enclosed in garlands of flowers, and the allegorical patterns which became so popular in America about 1800. He established a cotton print manufactory in the village of Jouy, near Versailles, and there the famous prints known as *toile de Jouy*—still a hallmark of fine decorative textiles—were made.

Toile de Jouy prints were first made entirely by the hand-block method. By 1770, however, cylinder printing had begun, so the output increased enormously. This also reduced the cost of the material to a point where the American Colonies could afford to bring it overseas on clipper ships, and establish a market for it in the New World. To capture this lucrative market, fabrics were decorated in typically American scenes, with allegorical heroes and historical events. One of the most popular of these was the "Four Continents"

Block printed cotton. Floral print (English) about 1815.

To make figure stand out from background design, stitch around main motif.

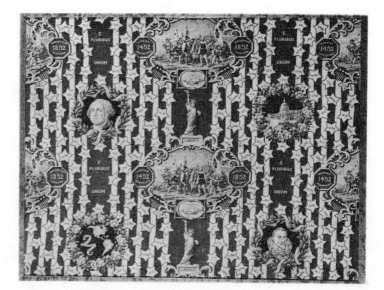

Alternating medallions of Statue of Liberty and Columbus discovering America. Head of George Washington and map of Americas to left; White House and other motifs to right.

Cotton printed in red, white and blue stripes and punctuated with various historical motifs—American (1892).

design. In this, the New World was placed on a par with Europe, Asia and Africa. Rural scenes showing modes of travel were also popular designs. These included steamboats, stagecoaches, Conestoga wagons and railroads.

The factory in Jouy employed many talented designers. The most famous and gifted of these was Jean-Baptiste Huet, who started working there in 1783. His designs are distinguished by architectural and geometric backgrounds, against which medallions and classical figures were placed. His textiles were permitted the use of the coat of arms of the King, as a trademark. If you have an original piece of toile-de-Jouy, look for the words *bon teint* on the selvage, meaning "fast dye."

Joseph-Marie Jacquard's contribution to the decorative arts was a power loom that could weave elaborate, colored designs into fabrics in imitation of hand-made patterns on brocades and cottons. The loom consisted of many heddles and harnesses, each of which could carry its own color thread—thus allowing a design of many colors.

A large textile plant was established in Manchester, England, and from that day to this, Manchester has remained the leader in England's great cotton industry. English-made flowered calicoes, muslins, and cambrics were the mainstay of American patchwork quilting from 1700 to 1885, before an American cotton industry became well established. The calicoes were woven in small motifs (known as "old-fashioned calico") and the colors had pleasant overtones of vivid reds, greens, yellows and blues.

Old Quilts for
Modern Decorating

In rooms which follow no special period in their decorating, as found in many new homes today, modern weaves and patterns are essential. Modern fabrics may also be used in many rooms which follow a definite period, depending on the elaborateness of the furnishings. With this in mind, we have selected three types of old quilts, which were in vogue 150 years ago, that might well be adapted to modern uses.

Since much of the charm of these quilts will depend on the fabric used, be sure to look around carefully before deciding on your fabric. You can start by looking through bureau drawers and trunks in your own home—perhaps you will find an old piece of chintz or toile you had forgotten about. Another good source is an antique shop or a thrift store in your vicinity. An old linen sheet (or a new one) makes a perfect top for a padded quilt on which to appliqué designs. Later, we will go into the procedures used in cutting out and applying

motifs from Indian prints. (Linen sheets make an excellent base for these!)

You will be able to find reproductions of many period patterns in your department store. If you do not see what you want in the fabric section, look among the draperies—you may find glazed chintz and the *toile de Jouy* patterns there.

WHITE QUILT WITH RAISED DESIGNS

White—that remarkable chameleon that changes its complexion to suit its surroundings—is attractive and pleasing in almost any setting. The foundation of a white quilt is fine muslin or linen, and its only ornamentation is a design quilted on its surface with the finest stitching possible. A loosely woven fabric covers the back so that after the quilting has been completed the motifs in the design can be emphasized by padding or stuffing them with bits of cotton.

Floral print—glazed cotton (English); mid-19th century.

A padded quilt can be made either by stitching two layers of fabric together (top and bottom) as in a counterpane—or by inserting a middle layer of cotton as in a regular quilt. The latter method is generally more satisfactory, since the padding and background stitches provide a firmer foundation and keep the quilt from wrinkling on the bed. The pattern used in quilting should be on a small scale—to contrast with the motifs in the main design. If these consist of curves, use geometric figures—straight lines, diamonds or squares, for example—for the quilting.

The designs used on old quilts usually had a distinctive central motif, such as a bunch of grapes, horn of plenty, or an American eagle. A border with matching motifs framed the entire quilt. After the quilting was completed, small holes were punched in the back of the quilt and tiny tufts of cotton were inserted from the rear with a crochet hook, to raise the design in appropriate places.

TEXTILE OR COMFORT QUILT

Another Colonial-type quilt was a counterpane or comforter of glazed chintz, with old rose, brown, green or yellow backgrounds. Patterns used at that time were printed on coarse fabrics which, when coupled with a thick inner layer of wool or cotton, and a home-spun lining, made the stitching necessarily coarse. English quilters used a fine backstitch that was so small and close it resembled machine stitching. By making a few changes in the quilting techniques, this type of quilt can serve two useful purposes today:

First—As a project for the beginning quilter who would like to learn to assemble a quilt and stitch the layers together. Stitching is done around the motifs in the design, eliminating the

Appliquéd basket of flowers, as central motif, framed with smaller baskets. Border trim is wool vine with offshoots of appliquéd flowers. Pennsylvania—early 19th century.

need for laying out a quilting pattern (generally a problem for the beginner).

Second—This type of quilt will satisfy the housewife whose purpose in making a quilt is to create a design that reflects her individuality and love of color. One need not always be traditional.

There is no limit to the individualized effects you can achieve if you shop around for the right fabric. There has been a tendency towards the use of abstract or geometric figures on textiles, to fit the decoration of modern homes with conventional furniture. If you are looking for a large, splashy motif—taken from nature—you will find both natural and abstract flower forms, tropical trees, and landscapes interspersed with brightly colored butterflies and birds.

Of course, one can find many of the *toile de Jouy* patterns charmingly reproduced in their original soft colors—plum, green, rose or blue. In using a Huet *toile de Jouy* print, stitch around the main characters only, ignoring the smaller units. This will emphasize the design— and require only half as much stitching as would otherwise be necessary. If you want a particular area to stand out, make a *double row* of stitching (about ½-inch apart) around it.

Or, if you want to create a playful mood, look for the new patterns which depict contemporary events in sports and games, such as riding, yachting, bathing, tennis, card playing, and picnicking—to name a few.

We have seen, recently, textiles with patterns which resemble old patchwork quilt patterns. The blocks are reproduced in every detail, even to patches of old-fashioned calico, in their original motifs and colors. We cannot quite approve of this type of design for a quilt top, however. We feel that quilt-making should remain a cherished art, full of tradition and dignity.

APPLIQUÉD REALISTIC DESIGNS

Here is another variety of quilts which has fallen into disuse, even though the techniques by which their charming effects are achieved are well known to quilting craftsmen. The ornamentation is based on cut-outs of flowers, trees, birds, and so forth, whose features were printed in a realistic fashion on the face of the textile. These motifs were cut away from the fabric, allowing a one-fourth margin all around, to be turned under for appliquéing. They were then arranged on a neutral background in whatever design the quilter had selected. This type of appliquéd design differs from those used today in that the pattern motifs are usually in a conventional or stylized form.

"The Tree of Life" was a popular Colonial

Tree of Life design.

pattern, not only because of its graceful branching and floral arrangements, but for its symbolic meaning. It was used as a basic design, extending the full length of the quilt. The trunk and branches were made of brown or green calico, on which were applied all kinds of leaves and flowers. To add interest, it was interspersed with colorful butterflies and birds. Sometimes the pattern was designed to represent a "family tree" which was personalized by adding symbols depicting the history of the family.

APPLIQUÉD INDIAN PRINT DESIGNS

In keeping with our idea that old quilts fit into new decorating schemes, we would like to suggest that a quilt top ornamented with cut-out motifs from an Indian print should look charming with furniture of any period. These prints are sold in most department stores today and are commonly used for bedspreads and in informal settings, such as family rooms or summer homes. The motifs in the designs are made up of exquisite colors—especially the reds and greens—which are identical with those used in Oriental rugs. If you want your quilt to follow the older tradition, apply the designs on to an off-white background, simulating the mellow effect of homespun cotton.

To appliqué motifs cut from a modern Indian print, first examine the weave. You will notice that the threads are quite coarse, so that there are fewer dents to the square inch. Such material, when cut, is likely to fray. Allow a wider margin around the motif as you cut, therefore, for turning in the edges.

The coarser fabric used in Indian prints also presents a sewing problem. When material is turned under, the edges become bulky, making the sewing somewhat more difficult. To simplify your task, therefore, use a tiny buttonhole stitch. An even easier way is to allow only $\frac{1}{8}$-inch of fabric beyond the outline of the design. Baste in position on top fabric, then sew on your sewing machine using a "satin stitch" attachment.

⧚⧚⧚⧚⧚⧚ SPECIAL-OCCASION QUILTS ⧚⧚⧚⧚⧚⧚

The special events which took place in a household, such as weddings, birthdays, new babies in the family, and so on, were the inspiration for many of the so-called "variety" quilts. Special-occasion quilts were also made as expressions of friendship, while others, of a seasonal nature (dark on one side and light on the other), were constructed for summer and winter use. These reversible quilts used the same type of fabric, in different shades, for the top and bottom.

The most elaborate of the quilts in this category were the Album and Presentation quilts. Blocks were exchanged, or given away, and each quilt-maker strove to produce a masterpiece in design and needlecraft.

ALBUM OR PRESENTATION QUILTS

As their name indicates, Album and Presentation quilts were made as expressions of friendship or admiration for a particular person. Often, the clergyman or an esteemed leader in a community was singled out to receive a gift quilt. The presentation of such quilts took place at a public gathering in which each block was presented personally by the donor. The quilt was then assembled and stitched together. Many of the blocks were signed by those who had worked on them—with the names cross-stitched or embroidered on (usually in color-fast red floss).

Album quilts have no specific pattern except that they are made in blocks or squares. Each block has a different design, created from materials selected by whoever made it. Motifs such as flowers, ferns, birds, trees, fruit, or hearts might appear on individual blocks which, when assembled and sewn together, created a pleasing and decorative effect. These quilts were seldom used for practical purposes, however, because of their elaborate designs. Many were carefully wrapped and stored, and taken out only on special occasions—as decorative pieces. Because they were so carefully protected, many of these old Album quilts are still in existence today, in museums and permanent collections.

Freedom Quilt. Quilted cotton coverlet—mid-19th century (American).

FRIENDSHIP QUILTS

These quilts were made by young women for purely social reasons. A "friendship medley party"—usually a surprise party—would be given by a girl's best friend. Each guest would fashion her own pattern from fabrics she had at home, and any materials that were needed for setting the blocks *together* would be supplied by the person giving the party. Every block in the completed quilt, therefore, would be different in design and color. Later, the girl for whom the medley party was given would reciprocate by inviting the same group to a quilting bee at *her* home.

FREEDOM QUILTS

Freedom quilts went out of fashion about 1825, but they are an interesting segment in the history of American quilts. In the early days of America, a boy's twenty-first birthday was a really special event. This probably carried over from a traditional custom in England which was observed especially in the case of an eldest son. It signified the time when a boy's parents or guardian could no longer bind him out as an apprentice; he was free to make decisions for himself.

Often, the boy's mother or sisters would invite girls of his acquaintance over for the afternoon and supper. The girls would bring scraps of fabric with them, from their prettiest gowns, and from such scraps they would piece a quilt for the young man. (This was actually for his future wife.) A party would follow, in the evening, at which the young man would appear in what was called his "freedom suit"—the first suit, probably, ever made especially for him.

BRIDES' QUILTS

Brides' dower chests years ago were supposed to contain at least a "baker's dozen" of quilts fashioned for everyday use. A *thirteenth* was a Bride's Quilt (made by the bride-to-be herself, following her engagement). The patterns and quilting designs used in Brides' Quilts were generally very elaborate. Simpler patterns were also used by the bride-to-be who was not especially skilled in needlework. The most popular pattern, probably, was the Rose of Sharon—a large pink rose surrounded by buds and foliage which was appliquéd on to a white background. Its name was probably derived from the Song of Solomon:

"I am the Rose of Sharon
And the Lily-of-the-Valley."

Because most brides adapted or varied the original design to suit their individual tastes, many versions of this pattern are available. The Lily-of-the-Valley pattern was not as popular as others (perhaps because the flower is white). One has only to look through an index of quilt names to find other wedding patterns: Double Wedding Ring; Bridal Stairway; Friendship Knot; Honeymoon Cottage, for example.

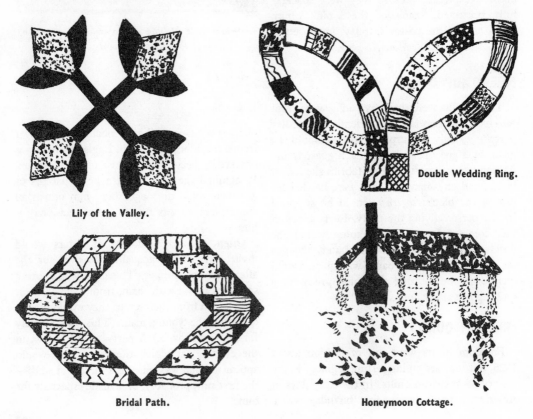

Lily of the Valley.

Double Wedding Ring.

Bridal Path.

Honeymoon Cottage.

Rose of Sharon.

89

Scene at a Pennsylvania Dutch quilt fair.

Some Practical and
Useful Suggestions

QUILTING FOR DECORATORS

Leisure time—so long the privilege of the few—has extended in recent years, and is now within the grasp of many, thanks to the development of time-saving devices in the home. It is natural, therefore, that some of this free time be used in a practical way. What better way than in needlework creations of your own design which can be sold! Since the craft of quilt-making progressed and developed when other textile arts in the home were declining, its durability as a practical art is apparent. Quilt-making, therefore, is the most logical choice in deciding on the kind of needlework to do in your free time. Creatively satisfying, its rewards extend from artistic achievement at one end to practical marketability at the other. One reason the marketing of quilts is sometimes difficult is that many of the designs, color schemes, and styles used are not easily adaptable to modern decoration. Some of the most successful quilters associate themselves with interior decorators who are professional designers—and these decorators supply the quilt fabrics which are best suited to the particular decoration of a room. There is a great need for quilters in the decorating field. If you are interested, contact interior decorators in your area for additional information.

QUILTING WORK AT HOME

There is always a demand for quilters who will do quilting in their own home. Many women enjoy piecing or appliquéing the quilt *top*, but do not want to bother with a quilting frame and prefer to have someone else do the quilting. You can advertise in local newspapers, church bulletins, antique magazines, and other appropriate places for quilters if you prefer to do only the top yourself. It is customary to charge according to the number of spools of thread used for the decoration. The price is

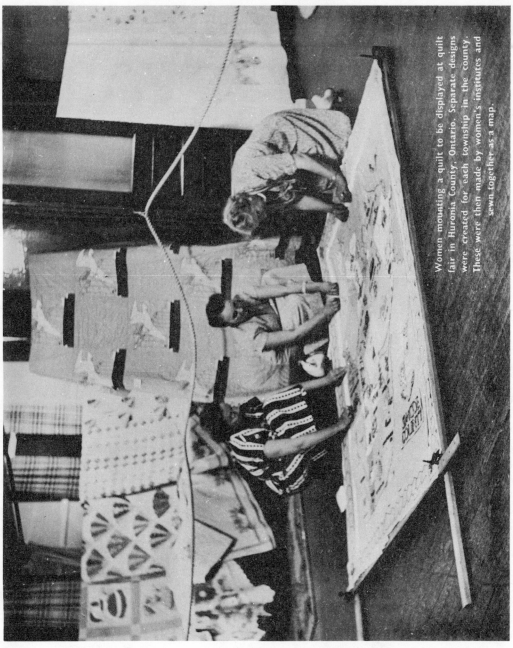

Women mounting a quilt to be displayed at quilt fair in Huronia County, Ontario. Separate designs were created for each township in the county. These were then made by women's institutes and sewn together as a map.

quoted as "so much a yard" but since each spool has a specific number of yards, it is easy to compute.

QUILTING IN GROUPS

In Colonial times, the quilting bee was an important social function. It combined pleasure with purpose, one of the rules set down by the Puritan Fathers. Some communities today still hold quilting parties—including a covered-dish luncheon or supper—but most group participation in quilting now takes place in churches or clubs where the purpose of such activity is to raise money for the organization in question. This is a splendid way to raise funds, and here are some practical suggestions to keep in mind in organizing a group activity of this kind.

First, a woman or committee of women familiar with all phases of quilt-making should be appointed to correlate the sewing of the various quilters, and assure production of a successful quilt.

Then, the quilters should be divided into groups of five: two to work on each side of the quilting frame, and a fifth to act as hostess. (Three women working on one side of a quilting frame is crowded!) Workers can quilt to a depth of 11 inches—then the quilt should be rolled back on the frame.

COMPETITIONS

There is nothing like competition to stimulate quilt-making in a community! Annual county fairs have always been an important factor in encouraging the art of quilt-making. Winning an annual fair prize for quilting was not only a notable reward but the many beautiful ex- amples displayed served to inspire other women to try their hand at this age-old craft.

For example, The National Quilt Contest, held at the Eastern States Exposition in Springfield, Massachusetts, is well known by quilt-makers throughout the United States. Every year, from 600 to 1,000 of America's finest quilts are displayed and prizes are awarded for quilts in various categories. Exhibitors include women who make quilts for commercial purposes, and those interested in quilting primarily as a craft. The competition also provides a positive program for locating talent among nonprofessional craftsmen.

QUILT FAIR

Each year, the quilt-makers of Huronia, Ontario, in Canada, hold a Quilt Fair. Because of its practicality for any county or community interested in setting up a similar event, we will discuss here the organization of this fair. Perhaps its program, which includes all the elements of sound community planning, co-operation and understanding (as well as financial know-how), will work just as successfully in your community!

Throughout the year, from October to the following August, committee members work together developing project ideas for the forthcoming fair. They may, in the past, have come across quilting designs depicting historical events of their immediate area, as well as native flora and fauna patterns. These, in the case of Huronia, included such items as trillium, lady slipper, Canada goose, swamp cabbage, trumpeter swan, and oxen and yoke.

The most novel pattern was the "Huronia Trail" which was made in a conventional design and used a cloud and canoe trail. Another striking all-over design illustrated a legend about an Indian who threw 30,000 islands into the Georgian Bay!

During the winter, committee members made a tour of about 100-mile radius, visiting groups, suggesting designs, and helping quilters with their particular problems. Quilt designs were exhibited in such remote places as store windows in tiny villages, while newspapers co-operated by supplying advertising space. One contributed posters, without charge, and radio stations carried interviews with committee members. Community spirit reached such a high point that even carpenters offered to make quilting frames, free of charge, for anyone who wanted them.

The Quilt Fair lasted three days. Articles for sale were exhibited in one area, while quilts made for display purposes only were in another. No prizes were awarded, but a feeling of good fellowship and congeniality prevailed, with everyone deeply interested in each other's work and achievements.

A unique and highly successful event, the fair proved how effective planning and community spirit could work together in displaying the talent and efforts of all who participated.

INDEX

95